CW00855383

Fred Eyre's first book, *Ki...* football classic. It is as popular and as educational to aspiring young footballers today as it was when it was first published in 1981.

Thanks to the written word, he was given the opportunity of *Taking the Mike*, by accepting countless invitations to travel the country to discuss his two favourite subjects – football and Fred Eyre!

As usual, his anecdotes and stories, written in his own unmistakable style, from within the game and from his career as one of the top sporting after-dinner speakers, make unusual, interesting and hilarious reading.

Also by Fred Eyre:

KICKED INTO TOUCH
ANOTHER BREATH OF FRED EYRE
WHAT A GAME!
STAR GAMES

Taking the Mike

Fred Eyre

WARNER BOOKS

A *Warner* Book

First published in Great Britain in 1991 by Futura Publications
Reprinted by Warner Books 1992
Reprinted 1996

ISBN 0 7515 0374 6

Typeset by Leaper & Gard Ltd, Bristol
Printed in England by Clays Ltd, St Ives plc

Warner
A Division of
Little, Brown and Company (UK)
Brettenham House
Lancaster Place
London WC2E 7EN

Contents

Acknowledgements

My thanks to Lynn Pye, whose fingers have travelled with me via the typewriter through five books. To Jerome Anderson Management, for prodding me into it and, of course, as ever to my family: Judith, Suzanne and Steven, Fred Snr and Muriel.

Thanks also to Paul Fletcher, Glen Buckley, Huddersfield Town Football Club and to Daniel Stocctiero, Stephen Thomas, Mark Wilson, Jason Byrne and Paul Thompson – I hope that they all enjoy long careers in the game. And finally thanks to John Rotherham and Bill Gibson.

Front cover photography by Christopher Neill.

Photographs by courtesy of:
Blackpool Gazette & Herald
Bolton Evening News
Christopher Neill
Adrian Ashurst
Bob Thomas Sports Photography
Paul Fletcher
Wilf Burrows
Denise Plum News Sport
Martin Birchall
The Sammy Nelson Collection by Monte Fresco
Richard Pacifico

Life's little luxuries

The success of *Kicked into Touch* changed the course of my whole life. Indeed, the autobiography of this little scrubber from north Manchester was so successful that I am now able to afford one or two of life's little luxuries that had hitherto been denied me during my formative years, where, in my day, if you wanted a new pair of shoes you went to the local swimming baths on a Saturday morning – it was as simple as that!

Necessities, such as football boots – Timpson Top Dog, of course – and food (in that order!) were never a problem. Dad was a butcher, so there was always some meat in the house, and Mother always insisted that I went to school with a good breakfast inside me. So it was porridge in the winter (when it was so cold and draughty in our little corporation houses that the wind often used to blow the locks off some of the gas meters!) and cornflakes every morning during those lovely long summers that we used to enjoy so much.

Even in those days I could not manage one Shredded Wheat, let alone three! Eating one of those things was like kissing Arthur Scargill on the head ... no thanks!

So it was good old cornflakes for me until the dreaded day, about once a fortnight, when we came to the last inch, where there is always a layer of itty-bitty bits that have dropped to the bottom quicker than the *Titanic*.

I simply hated to eat that final bowl, the thought of it even now makes me feel like throwing up, but those little flakes could not be wasted; they had to be eaten before a new packet of fresh, crisp, huge flakes could be opened. That is how things were in Blackley. But nowadays, thanks to *Kicked into Touch* and my newly acquired status in posh Worsley (where they even have fruit on the sideboard when nobody is ill), I can, with a theatrical flourish reminiscent of Lord Olivier in *Othello*, or of Maradona in the World Cup, simply fling the packet, bits and all, into the waste bin, without giving it a second thought.

Now *that* is my idea of a comfortable lifestyle. Damn the expense! I hear that Donald Trump used to do exactly the same thing in Atlantic City ... but not any more, now that Ivana wants her half of the bits!

I will admit to a slight twinge of conscience even now, as the bin lid slams shut again; occasionally, a vision of my Mother flashes before my eyes: she is standing there with her hands thrust deeply into the pouch of her pinny, wearing only one stocking if it was Friday – she always made suet pudding on a Friday morning! But the apparition passes quickly and I sit back, relax and start the day in style.

I considered myself to be one of the fortunate ones, to be brought up on our sprawling council estate in the late 1940s and the 1950s – and I am still proud of where I came from, and I like to go back there as often as possible ... I like to visit my hub caps now and again! It is fashionable these days, of course, to be environmentally friendly, but Blackley has always been that way. All the churches in our area have been unleaded for as long as I can remember!

I was lucky to attend a school like Crosslee Primary School; it is still there today, nestling behind Blackley's

2

most famous pub, the Clough Hotel. The local lads still go there and they all love it, because it reminds them of the Blackley of old.

Crosslee was run by our eccentric headmistress, Miss Helen Stone, who was really a couple of generations ahead of her time. Teachers were not allowed to smack the pupils at Crosslee ... but it was OK for the kids to knock seven bells out of the teachers though! Despite being the only school that I was aware of with this policy, the disciplinary record at Crosslee was almost exemplary, because none of us ever wanted to let Miss Stone down, or to be summoned to her office for 'a little chat'.

She cycled to school each morning, waving to everybody in sight, left and right like the Queen, wearing her weird clothes, always topped off by a purple beret with matching lipstick. A purple circle of rouge the size of a half-crown on each cheek completed the vision – teaching's answer to Margaret Rutherford, and she was loved and respected by everyone. If only life could have continued like that, with adults following the principles of Crosslee Primary School, the world would definitely be a better place in which to live.

Many years later, I was invited back to Crosslee as guest of honour by the current headmaster, Mr Kundi, to present the end-of-year prizes celebrating the school's golden jubilee. It turned out to be one of the most memorable days of my life. When I consider the number of pupils who had passed through the doors of this great school (over what must have been about 50 years!), for them to ask me, the lad from Clough Top Road, made me feel very proud indeed.

Miss Stone had sadly long since passed away by this time, but after the ceremony I drove round the corner to have a peep at the block of flats that had been named after her, and it saddened me to see two of the letters missing from her name and one wall covered in

3

graffiti. 'Kilroy' obviously was not a Crosslee Boy, otherwise he would have thought twice about defacing the walls of Helen Stone House. I am sure that I was not invited back because of my excellence with the three Rs during my time at the school. If it had been the three Fs I could have understood it: football, football and forgetting my dinner money!

It was the success of *Kicked into Touch* that did it. It would appear that the public, while appreciating the life stories of footballing superstars, were also beginning to find the rags-to-riches biographies a little old hat.

Each player seemed to have been spotted, while kicking a ball of rags against the wall of the end terraced house, by a kindly old scout wearing a flat cap with a bag of sweets in the pocket of his trusty old overcoat. The lad's mother always used to pay the cobbler much more each week than she did to the butcher, because her soccer-daft son was always kicking the toes out of his only pair of shoes. But how well it all turned out in the end, as that very same boy, some ten years later, slipped out of his Gucci hand-sewn little numbers, popped them under his seat in the spacious dressing room at Wembley Stadium and slid his million-pound feet into a top-of-the-range pair of sponsored Pumas, while at the same time pulling an England jersey over his coiffured head.

Unfortunately, life, for most of us, is not like that. While the truth often hurts, it is true to say that my experiences, chronicled quite honestly, were easier for the average person in the street to relate to, as this soccer-mad kid came unstuck along the way.

Kicked into Touch opened so many different doors for me, I only wish that I had learned the combination quite a few years earlier. In fact, so salubrious had life become, that some doors would mysteriously swing wide open as I simply ambled towards them. I did not even have to knock, let alone hammer or try to break them down. It was all so different from my early days when the crest on the Eyre coat of arms seemed to read: 'Quo uno dooro closo ... ano uno smashi da moosh' (Professor Stanley Unwin, 1967). Roughly translated this means: 'When one door closes ... another one slams in your face.'

Now, due to this simple little tome, certainly not to be found on the shelf marked 'Modern Classics', and even more difficult to obtain than *Fly Fishing* by JR Hartley (good old *Yellow Pages*!), I had in one fell swoop become a sports broadcaster with my own spot – well, more of a blemish really – every morning on Piccadilly Radio's Breakfast Show with the wonderful Dave Ward, the crazy Timmy Mallett and the turbo-charged Andy Crane, before he opted for his now-famous broom cupboard on children's TV.

I became a 'journalist' at the *Daily Express*, with my own weekly column which became so popular that the more militant members of the National Union of Journalists decided that I would have to go ... pretty quickly. Not that such a thing bothered me too much – I did not ask to write the articles, I was invited to do so by the sports editor, presumably because he thought I could do a better job than his own trained men. After all I did once get a tick for composition at Ducie Avenue High School for Boys!

No! I did not lose any sleep over that little confront-ation and, anyway, a quick chapter from *Kicked into Touch* would have been enough to cure even the severest bout of insomnia.

Finally, I became an after-dinner speaker, an after-lunch speaker, an after-hot-pot (with red cabbage) speaker and, occasionally, after some of the food that has been served up to me, an after-Alka-Seltzer speaker.

I have spoken to prisoners in jail, a captive audience

if ever there was one, received a standing ovation from the Haemorrhoids Society, and lectured to the Retired Teachers' Association, where the entire front row was taken up with my ex-teachers from Ducie Avenue. It unsettled me for a few moments, thinking that in years gone by it was they who had lectured to me and now, for this one day, the roles were to be reversed. This could be a tricky one, I thought, but they were very attentive, very kind and only gave me a hundred lines at the end.

While I was in full flow, my eye fell upon one of my less favourite teachers of my day, and immediately my mind flew back to the time I lost my bus fare – or, more likely, I had spent it on an Arrow Bar or a Trebor Chew – and asked him if he would lend it to me until the following morning.

'How much is it?' he asked.

'One shilling and three pence, sir.' (It was an hour, and three buses, from school in Moss Side to home in Blackley.)

I could picture the scene as clearly now, from the stage, as I could at the time.

'How much?' he bellowed. 'Where do you live, boy? Edinburgh? Here's sixpence ... walk the rest of the way.'

It was November, lashing down with rain, the Phillips-stick-a-sole on my shoe had come unstuck. If I had trodden on a half-crown, I could have told you whether it was heads or tails. My sock felt like a trainer's sponge as I traipsed miserably up Rochdale Road, past the billiard hall which is now Bernard Manning's World Famous Embassy Club, through Boggart Hole Clough to home.

It was 7.30 when I finally arrived home; my Mother was beside herself with worry, but recovered quickly enough to batter me around the house. My tea was cooling off in the dustbin and, taking things all round,

6

it had been a bad end to the day. All in all, that little hole in my pocket, or my liking for goodies from the tuckshop, had given me a few problems, and now I was focusing on the cause of it, sitting beaming at me from the front row of the stalls, completely unaware of the grief he had once caused me. Still, that was all water into my shoe.

I had exchanged his classroom for the Manchester City dressing room, just as I had hoped that I would. As far as I was concerned, everything was going according to plan and I paid little attention to his parting shot: 'Well, good luck Eyre, but God help you, if ever your feet let you down.' If he listened carefully during the next half an hour, he would get some idea just how much those feet of mine actually did let me down, but I managed to have a bit of fun along the way.

As a young professional, some of my experiences at the hands of my managers and coaches are still too painful to recall, but, as I matured into the veteran stage and my business interests grew with me, I was able to relax a little and enjoy a laugh at my own expense. I have certainly had enough practice. One of my managers began to question my ability to last the full 90 minutes and thought that it would be good tactics to substitute me after 70 minutes, and bring on a fresh, young pair of legs for the final 20 minutes of the game. I did not think that this was a very good idea at all, but, in the immor(t)al words of Mandy Rice Davies, 'I wouldn't, would I?'

Undeterred, he proceeded to hook me off before the end for six consecutive games, until I decided to do something about it. Just before we left the dressing room to start the second half, I nicked the 'Number 3' card from his set of numbers, hid it in the toilet and thoroughly enjoyed myself for the second period of the game, until I saw our trainer standing on the touchline, 20 minutes from the end, holding the white inside of

7

an Elastoplast box aloft, with '3' scribbled on it in biro. When they want you off that badly, you just have to go as gracefully as possible!

In this book I am 'Taking the Mike', it is true ... but there are no prizes for guessing out of who!!

CHAPTER I

Hats off to Larry

Wigan Athletic had just beaten Port Vale quite comfortably at Springfield Park and I, as assistant manager, was feeling quite pleased with my little self. I thought that, as well as displaying a fair degree of professionalism during a hectic second half, when we had survived a distinctly dodgy spell with a mixture of canny defensive play and pure undiluted experience at the heart of the defence in the shape of Colin Methven and player/manager Larry Lloyd, we had also demonstrated that, creatively, the team that Larry and I had put together would be more than a match for any team in the fourth division.

Indeed, I felt confident enough to make that very point to the little throng of journalists who always gathered in the manager's office after the game to jot down the usual boring managerial meanderings and post-match clichés that we have all heard a million times before. It is an accepted part of the manager's job these days, dissecting the previous 90 minutes for the benefit of the press boys, making their job easier for the next day's nationals. Repeating outrageous post-match quotes is a lot easier than actually watching the game.

Like most other things in football, Bill Shankly started the ball rolling in his Liverpool days, but the difference is that Shanks always had something interesting to say as he held court in the now-famous Anfield boot room, whereas most managers in the same situation have very little to offer to the done-it-all, seen-it-all, hard-bitten scribes gathered around them.

I did not much look forward to these confrontations every Saturday afternoon at 4.45. Larry Lloyd was the manager, but, as he was still active on the playing side, he was invariably soaking his aching limbs in the bath at this time, so the responsibility usually fell to me to entertain the press in the little office we both shared.

When I say 'office', I use the term very loosely indeed. It was a room the size of an average airing cupboard, tucked away at the bottom of a dimly lit corridor, sandwiched beautifully between the players' toilet on one side and the public conveniences on the other. A marvellous piece of planning by the ground committee to position it there at the outset and, indeed, when the manager was in residence, it was said repeatedly by the players that there were three such receptacles all in a row!

'Thank you, gentlemen,' I said in conclusion. I had talked plenty but said nothing, just like all the rest, but the press gang seemed happy enough. As I skipped niftily out into the corridor, I was just in time to hear what I took to be the sound of crockery smashing against a wall. I knew that there was no Greek banquet taking place in our dressing room and was about to investigate further when one of the goalscorers, right back John McMahon, limped past me on his weekly pilgrimage to the treatment room.

'What's all the noise about?' I enquired.

John never checked his painful stride, did not raise his voice, nor flicker an eyebrow and said, quite matter-of-factly: 'It'll probably be Larry throwing the cups about.'

We were barely a third of the way through the

season and already the players were resigned to Larry's wild outbursts and, while it was a frightening sight to witness one of Larry's specials in full flight, they were happening so often, that now they were not making any impact on the players whatsoever. I could not imagine what dastardly deed had incurred his wrath on this occasion, possibly it could have been something really serious, like somebody forgetting to put sugar in his tea, or maybe he was simply playing the role of super-perfectionist, whereby even though we all knew that the team, Larry included, had just played very well, he was too long in the tooth, too wily a campaigner to be totally satisfied with any performance and that there was always something to be improved upon, no matter how well the team thought it had played.

Whatever it was, I too was getting a bit brassed off with it and the cracks were beginning to show, as I began to spend less and less time in the office with Larry after training and more time in the dressing room with the players, where I felt more comfortable ... and safe!

We had already had to suffer the embarrassment of starting the second half of a game against Bourne-mouth with only ten men, because Larry had substi-tuted two players at half time. This, of course, was in the days when only one substitute was allowed. As soon as we reached the dressing room at the end of the first half, he banished strikers Tony and Mickey Quinn to the bath, after what he obviously considered to be a below-par performance from the pair of them. It was not until Larry and the other nine players were on the pitch that I nipped back into the dressing room to fish a Quinn (Mickey) out of the bath. I helped him back into his kit and, even though he was still dripping wet, I pushed him back onto the field, seven minutes into the second half, pausing only to give his thigh an imaginary final rub, in an attempt to make the crowd

11

think that I had been treating him for a pulled muscle.

What was I going to do with Larry?

The answer, of course, was nothing. He was the boss: strong-willed, single-minded, explosive and uncontrollable, except when chairman Freddie Pye was around. So, if there were any adjustments to be made, I would have to be the one to make them and, at first, because I was totally convinced that Wigan Athletic would win promotion that season, I thought that possibly, just possibly, I might be able to rearrange my principles a little, just long enough to help guide the club into the third division for the first time in their short football league history.

It was a long time since I had come across such a complex character as Larry Lloyd. In our private moments, I found him to be pleasant, if somewhat moody, company, but in front of the players, it was usually a different matter and he never wasted a chance to give them a little bit of stick.

There were times, however, like our week's stay at Exeter University, when the mood needed lightening and he tried occasionally to become 'one of the lads' again by joining in the general banter. The players soon cottoned on to this and one player in particular used to make provocative remarks to the rest of the squad, in a voice just loud enough for him to hear, as Larry strode by: 'He stayed out all last night you know.'

'Who did?' demanded Larry.

'The Man in the Moon,' the joker chortled as Larry took a deep breath and walked away.

A couple of days later, it was the same scene: 'He's definitely "bent" if you ask me.'

'Who is?' said Larry.

'The man in a suitcase.' More chortling from the lads.

Larry summoned me to his room: 'Tell him to cut it out,' he said. 'I don't like it.'

'OK,' I replied, 'but it's only a bit of fun.'

After dinner that evening, I spoke to the players and warned them of dire consequences if the boss baiting did not stop. They grumbled a bit, but agreed to be sensible until a couple of days later, when the entire squad was dossing about watching the Test match in the television lounge, which was situated on the ground floor – which was just as well as things turned out.

Larry came down the stairs looking immaculate in a full white tracksuit, except for the Nottingham Forest emblem of a tree picked out in red on the breast. We had trained hard that morning, he had showered and, in that European Cup-winning gear, he looked the picture of health: 'What's the score?' he asked of nobody in particular.

All eyes remained glued to the screen as one of them piped up: 'He's one off 50.'

I held my breath. No, surely not! They would not dare. Right on cue Larry replied: 'Who is?'

Oh, my God! Here it comes, I thought. It was like an Exocet missile – I could see it coming, but there was nothing I could do about it!

'PC49,' the lad shrieked, jumped out of his chair, punched the air with delight and leaped through the window.

Larry gave me one of his looks, and I shrugged my shoulders apologetically.

The end was not long in coming. Another home performance against league leaders Torquay United again did not satisfy Larry, who proceeded to lambast his midfield players at the end of the game. They were the very three players whose extra efforts, in my opinion, had eventually managed to wrestle the game our way and had been the most influential in getting us a good result.

I convinced myself that this roasting was nothing to do with me as I moved among the players, collecting

13

the odd tie-up or shin-pad off the dressing-room floor. Most of them looked uncomfortable for the three lads who were taking all the stick, because they knew that they did not deserve it. One of them caught my eye as I busied myself with these imaginary jobs and he just rolled his eyes up into his forehead and shook his head sadly as we waited for the storm to subside, before diving into the bath.

Finally, the moment came. With the panache of a male stripper at a Thursday night hen party, Larry whipped off his jock-strap, threw it dramatically onto the dressing-room floor, which was a relief, and headed for the bathroom.

If that had been the end of the matter, yet another crisis would have been allowed to evaporate, like the steam now rising from the bath and from Larry's ears, but, as he drew level with me, I think even Larry must have been momentarily stunned by the deafening silence that had embarrassingly descended on a dressing room that only minutes earlier had been bubbling with the excited chatter and noise of victory and, as such, he felt moved to enlist my support of his criticisms of the players concerned.

This was it. The moment my credibility, my honesty and my character were put on the line. I had a fraction of a second to make up my mind which way to jump. I could feel the eyes of all the players upon me as Larry stood alongside me, totally naked, his huge, sweaty, right shoulder level with my left earhole, as we faced the whole dressing room. I could see it in their faces, they were mentally taking bets. Will he? Or won't he?

They would all have understood if I had sided with the boss. This would have enabled me to join the long list of survivors, men who have remained in the game all their lives, at various clubs throughout the football league, by simply always agreeing with the manager. But I knew that I could not compromise myself, and I

14

did not let them, or myself, down.

I knew that Larry would never forgive me for not supporting him, but there was no way, no matter how much I loved the club, that I was going to become a parasite of the game. No way that I was going to play the 'Yes/No interlude', as your quiz inquisitor Michael Miles used to call it. I could not swallow my pride by saying 'Yes', when my head, my heart and my soul were all screaming 'No!'. That is not for me. I was always going to give an honest appraisal of any situation, even though manager Larry Lloyd did tell me within seconds of my appointment as his assistant: 'Don't ever disagree with me in public. If you don't like something, just swallow it and wait until we get back to the office.'

I nodded in agreement at the time, thinking that it was a fair enough deal and, quite honestly, I thought that I would have no difficulty keeping my end of the bargain.

I was wrong!

It did not take me long to collect my gear from the office and, one hour after the final whistle, I walked out of Springfield Park for the last time. But obviously the penny did not drop with the manager, because it was not until the following Tuesday that he rang me at my shop in Manchester and told me not to travel with the team to Aldershot that day – he did not even know that I had gone!

I had obviously been sadly missed.

CHAPTER 2

Beware the man who is everybody's friend

In all honesty it was no great problem for me to quit as Larry's assistant. If there is one thing that I cannot stand in football, it is the young assistant whose desire to stay in the game is so great that he will do absolutely anything and agree with every single thing in order to do so. We all know who they are, they are known to supporters up and down the country as 'loyal servants', but are generally regarded by everybody inside their respective clubs as total creeps and there was no way that I was going to add my name to that growing list.

Do not get me wrong. They are not all like that. I admire loyalty like everybody else, but not at the expense of self-respect. There is nothing that I like better than to sit and listen to some of the game's elder statesmen, the ones with their own individual views on the game, which they are not afraid to express. You can tell, just by listening to them, that they have always been their own man.

I remember sitting in the lounge of a hotel just off the East Lancs Road one afternoon with a first division manager and his right-hand man. The boss said that he was thinking of putting in a sizeable bid for a goal-

16

keeper, so he had obviously taken a liking to the lad. As an afterthought, he asked his assistant what he thought of him. Without hesitation he shocked his boss by replying: 'If you centred a bale of hay, he wouldn't manage to get a handful.'

I was impressed with his honesty and allowed myself a quiet chuckle. I made a mental note that here indeed was future managerial material, and the assistant is in fact now a top first division manager in his own right. And quite right too.

It is difficult to imagine that, in a profession like football, with such a cross-section of people from perfect gentlemen to out-and-out toe-rags, how anybody can work alongside a dozen different managers over a period of time at one club and be on good terms and in total agreement with all of them, all of the time. Surely he could not have been bosom pals with them all.

There are indeed those who have actually been the manager of a club, then demoted through the ranks from top to bottom and back again because nobody quite knows what to do with them. They will potter about the ground, growl at the young kids and generally scuffle about, contributing next to nothing, until the wheel eventually turns another notch, another manager becomes a statistic and they find themselves back in harness again – until the next time. And all simply because they swallowed the lot and kept their noses clean. It is so embarrassing to see.

Indeed, I once asked the vice-chairman of one club what the current position was of a former manager, now that he had been relieved of his managerial duties and been replaced by a new manager, but had remained on the staff.

'He's now in charge of the tea bags,' I was told.

Well that just about sums it up. At between £20,000 and £30,000 a year, I am sure that some of the paying spectators would be delighted to hear that, or even exchange jobs with him.

There are those, of course, with football running through their blood, who recognize the passing of time, feel the old bones creaking a bit and move on to the physiotherapy side of the game. Great! They go to Lilleshall, pass a little exam and treat the not-too-serious injuries with a mixture of a little knowledge, great humour, wonderful warmth and above all a deep love of the game.

Of course, years ago, the trainer had to do the physio's job as well at most fourth division clubs, and this was the case during my time at Lincoln City, where I had the opportunity to spend many hours·in deep conversation with Bill McGlen while he was pummelling me on the table in the dingy little treatment room in the far corner of Sincil Bank.

I am not saying that I was injury-prone, but during that season at Lincoln I was on the treatment table so often that they needed a welder's torch to prise me off it. So I had plenty of opportunity to get to know Bill very well, and he became one of my favourite characters and, in me, he had a great ally, a fresh-faced, ultra-keen, impressionable 19-year-old who latched onto and absorbed his every word.

Bill did not always make things easy for me to understand however. He just used to pull me to one side ... and leave me there! And he had his own peculiar way of 'gannin aboot' things. His Geordie accent was not always easy to comprehend either, though I usually managed to get the general drift of things. But not always.

'Sometimes, you know Fred, principles can be costly things,' he said with a sad shake of the head one afternoon, when the ground was empty except for him and me. The players had gone home after training and I was the only player on the injured list, the only one back for treatment. It was a miserable day; the rain was beating a tattoo on the corrugated tin roof and he was brewing up.

We were ready for one of our discussions.

As usual, in those distant days, when my hair was bright red, thick and wavy, when my waist was a trim 28 inches, and I could jump out of bed in the mornings without my right knee buckling underneath me, I nodded knowingly.

'Dead right,' I agreed, not having the faintest idea then what he was talking about. I do now, of course, and I did as soon as I began to contemplate my departure from Wigan Athletic. I knew what I was giving up. I knew I was waving goodbye to a side heading for certain promotion and all the ecstasy that goes with it. I knew that I was giving up an enjoyable life with the players, full of fun and dressing-room banter. I also knew that there would be no turning back.

Of course, people said it was easy for me to hold such idealistic opinions from the comfort of a luxurious house in one of the upper-class areas of Manchester, from behind the wheel of a gleaming, top-of-the-range Mercedes, from behind the executive desk of one of the most successful commercial stationery businesses in the north of England. But they obviously did not know me as well as they thought they did, because I can honestly say that even if I was down to my last piece of Beech Nut chewing gum, my ideals and opinions would not change. Most of my old trainers must have encountered this dilemma at some time, or indeed many times, during their lifetimes in the game. What did they do?

Well, they stayed in the game, didn't they? And good luck to them. I respect the old-timers much more than the so-called good clubmen of today, who sit on the fence so much their backsides must be red raw at the end of each game. At the moment the game is chock-a-block with people, both in the game and on the periphery, who are picking up wages simply because they do not rock the boat or make waves, and they do nothing to disrupt the status quo as they nod and shake their heads so vigorously in all the right places that their nappers must be in grave danger of toppling off. They hang on in there, respected by nobody, but prepared to put up with anything, simply to remain in football. If ever the four-minute warning goes off, just find one of these men at your local football club and stand next to him, you are certain to survive.

No! Give me the old-timer every time, he stayed in the game because he loved it, the game meant more to him than anything else, the fact that it was his job was simply regarded as a bonus. It is like the old geezer in the circus, who has been following the elephants around the ring for 60 years with a brush and shovel, sweeping up the elephant droppings. He was interviewed on his 75th birthday by the local reporter: 'You've been doing this same horrible job now for 60 years, don't you think it's time to call it a day?'

'What! And give up show business?!'

Costly things principles? We'll see.

CHAPTER 3

An old pair of trainers

The old trainers are a breed apart, but sadly they are almost extinct these days, like left halves and publicity-shy directors. Clubs simply cannot afford to carry them on the staff and certainly the game is poorer for the fact that they are no longer a part of it.

I wish that I could say the same thing about the new-style, high-profile, ball-juggling directors nowadays. They sign as many autographs as the players. Recently I was asked to compère the Miss Manchester United beauty contest and, even though it was a new departure for me, I was happy to oblige, because my good friend Vince Miller, the usual man for the job, had been suddenly laid low with a serious illness and, despite my allegiance to the sky-blue half of Manchester, United have always been very good to me, so I was delighted to step in at the last minute.

I arrived at Old Trafford and was ushered through to commercial manager Danny McGregor's plush office for a run-through prior to the event, just like Michael Aspel and Eric Morley used to do. In fact Eric, I believe, would have done the job himself but his hair was having an oil change! The usual team photographs and souvenirs were much in evidence; it was an Aladdin's cave for any United-mad youngster, and along the back wall of his office was a line of a dozen spanking new footballs, each one personally autographed by the United players. Bryan Robson, Mark Hughes, Brian McClair – they were all there. Jim Leighton had not signed them, but I believe that he got a touch to each one as they were passed around the dressing room! And there, among that galaxy of stars, taking up a full panel of each ball, in bold black felt pen was the signature of Michael Knighton.

My stomach turned over.

Manchester United, as I say, have been very good to me. I will never forget their kindness when I sustained a very nasty Achilles' tendon injury a few years ago, the type of problem that put Neil Webb out of action for almost a full season and has indeed ended the careers of many players in the past. This type of injury is difficult enough to overcome if you are a fit young player, but to pick up one at my age was very bad news indeed.

With manager Ron Atkinson's full permission, the Reds' physio Jim McGregor gave me specialist treatment every single day for four months, until I had fully recovered. He organized a special shoe for me to wear that prevented me aggravating the injury again and also supervised my remedial training once he had declared me fit enough to jog and run again – in my case fit enough simply to jog!

I would arrive fairly early each morning at The Cliff, United's superb training headquarters in Salford, and Jim would treat me like the star I never was, to quite embarrassing proportions. First-team players like Frank Stapleton and Lou Macari would come in and ask for their ankles to be strapped, and Jim would send them away with a dismissive wave of the hand: 'Come back in ten minutes. I'm just seeing to Fred.' And off they would trot, while I cringed with embarrassment.

Robbo would put his head round the door hoping for

another quick, major operation! Kevin Moran would do the same thing, asking for the usual quota of stitches to be inserted in his face, only to be sent packing the same way. One morning Kevin really gave Jim a shock. He came in with 385 stitches covering his face ... he had put his balaclava on back to front!

'Jim,' I whispered eventually. 'You know I've got all day, if you want to sort the players out first.'

Jim just laughed: 'It won't do 'em any harm to wait a few minutes once in a while ... anyway you're twice as old as they are.'

Jim McGregor was absolutely fantastic to me, so much so that, a few months later, when the inevitable happened, and the Achilles in my other leg snapped, the exact same, serious injury, I did not have the heart to let him know that I was struggling yet again.

It stands to reason really: I had had both Achilles for the same length of time, both doing the same amount of work, taking the same strain, so it is odds-on that if one snaps then, within a short period of time, the same thing is going to happen to the other one, but I knew that if he found out, he would treat me in exactly the same way all over again and United's injured star players would never get fit!

My constant companion on the other treatment table during this period was Republic of Ireland international Paul McGrath, recovering from yet another operation on his fragile knees. Paul, as well as being one of the world's great players, is a lovely lad, with a quiet whispery voice that quite belies his muscular frame. He is easygoing, good-natured, good company and quite enjoys being the target of the quick humour of the other players.

This particular morning, he and I were in our usual prone positions, while Jim busied himself around the treatment room. Macari, who has an impish sense of humour, came in for a plaster, pointed his finger accusingly at McGrath and said: 'Jim, I think it's only right to tell you that he hasn't done his running this morning.'

Before Jim could reply, the Irishman said indignantly:

'I have so, I've done the 12-minute run that Jim told me to do.'

'How long did it take you?' Macari answered with a smile.

'I felt really good this morning,' said Paul. 'I did it in under nine minutes.'

'Well done,' said Lou, with a straight face.

'Yes! You're obviously nearing full fitness now,' said Jim.

I looked round at the three of them and could not decide who was taking the mickey out of whom!

A few days later Jim decided that Paul's knee was strong enough for some extra exercise. 'Right,' he said, fingering the offending joint, 'I want you to do "the alphabet" for me.' He then proceeded to show McGrath the exercise in question.

'A straight leg raise into four different positions: one, two, three, four – that's "A". Same again: one, two, three, four – that's "B". And again – that's "C", until you go right through the alphabet, which will make 104 straight leg raises in total. OK?' said Jim.

'Fine,' nodded Paul as he set to work. We both watched him for a few minutes: straight leg raise – one, two, three, four – 'A'. Straight leg raise – one, two, three, four – 'B'. Jim was satisfied that Paul knew what he was supposed to be doing and turned his attention back to me. We both remained faintly aware of a soft Irish brogue mumbling in the background: 'One, two, three, four – "C". One, two, three, four –"D".'

After a short while, however, we both realized that the counting had ceased. Jim stopped massaging my leg, looked at me quizzically and turned round to see

24

Paul, face contorted with the sheer exertion of the exercise, leg still in the outright position, sweat popping out on his forehead, he just about managed to gasp between clenched teeth: 'What comes after "T"?'

This was bad enough, but at that moment, young Welsh international Alan Davies, recovering from a broken leg, limped into the room, without a clue what anybody was talking about and said: '*Coronation Street*, isn't it?'

I was almost sorry when Jim eventually declared me fit for the outside world again, I had forgotten just how much I had been missing.

Jim McGregor is, of course, at the very peak of his chosen profession. He is familiar with all the modern devices and techniques that are now available to a club like Manchester United in order to get their star players back onto the pitch in double-quick time, so that the club can get some return on its massive cash outlays. Their equivalents in the early days, however, were not quite of the same advanced standards. But the players loved them just the same, even though, in some cases, they were ruining careers instead of saving them, simply because they really did not know what they were doing. They were, however, experts at touching up X-rays, so that you could not see the break – and that was before Tippex was even invented!

They used to wear their woollen mufflers high under their chin (or chins!), their ordinary baggy flannels tucked into their woolly socks, great big, old-fashioned, ankle-high football boots, with scarred, steel toecaps bearing the traces of dried blood. No Timpson Top Dog for them. They had horny fingers, skin like leather, they could crack walnuts with their fingers and when they pressed those fingers into your hamstrings, they could dig deep enough to twang 'em like Hank Marvin. But they all had one thing in common: they all had hearts of gold and they were always chipping away at

25

me, giving me little gems of advice, pearls of wisdom to try to make me a better player.

They never actually spelled things out for me – it is a pity that they did not, I might have progressed a bit further in the game as a player, they just gave me broad hints and expected me to work out the finer details for myself.

By the time I did, it was too late; the game had virtually passed me by. But, to be fair, none of them ever gave up on me. They must have known in their hearts that I was a sad case, that I had no chance whatsoever, but they would not pack in with me, and they were always at me, pushing and prodding to try to improve my game.

If only the managers, the men whose opinions really counted, could have shown the same patience, things might have turned out a little better, but managers are yet another different kettle of fish altogether.

It is absolutely staggering how players change when they exchange the tracksuit for the double-breasted pin-stripe. Lads who simply hated long-distance running, for example, and moaned and rebelled at the very mention of the word, when they moved onto the administrative side of the game and the manager's sign went up on their door, albeit in chalk, five-a-sides were out and it was run rabbit run.

Frank McLintock, Arsenal's great double-winning captain and marvellous motivator as well as a super player, was one who loved to talk football with the team at any opportunity, always looking to improve things and to help other players get a little more out of their game. Nowadays, he has a laugh with his best pal George Graham, and says that in their playing days together it was always George who was forever putting a friendly arm round his shoulders saying: 'Put the ball away Frank, let's unwind a little, have another drink.'

Now, of course, George is the tough disciplinarian boss of Highbury.

As a kid I used to admire the skills of Don Revie when he graced the turf at Manchester City – that was when he was not in dispute with the club, of course. He was a lovely passer of the ball and, in tandem with Ken Barnes, another marvellous player, they passed their way around the Maine Road pitch to their hearts' content. It was a joy to watch for youngsters like me, with aspirations to play the game at that level. It was while watching those two pass-masters week after week that I came to the firm opinion that passing is the most important thing in football – at least it was in those days. At the moment, a pair of lungs like two barrage balloons and legs like tree trunks are also a big help, but, as far as I'm concerned, if you cannot pass, you cannot play. It is as simple as that.

Revie certainly could pass, but the physical side of the game was something quite abhorrent to him. However, when he constructed his great Leeds United team of the 1960s and 1970s, in conjunction with the stars who could play and pass, the team also contained a sprinkling of players who, shall we say, enjoyed the physical aspect of the game as well, and were not averse to autographing one or two shins during the course of 90 minutes.

Indeed, I spoke to Don shortly after he had returned to England following his defection to the United Arab Emirates, but before that tragic illness took a grip on his life, and I asked him what was so special about his great team. Surprisingly, he did not mention the leadership of Bremner, the passing of Giles, the aerial dominance of Jack Charlton or the left feet of Hunter and Cooper. He never spoke about the venom of Lorimer's shooting, the dribbling of Eddie Gray, the ... well, he did not mention Paul Reaney either! Nor the versatility of Paul Madeley. The goal-poaching of Allan

Clarke was overlooked, together with the industry of Mick Jones and Gary Sprake's handling – thank goodness!

He paused briefly, obviously enjoying this moment of nostalgia. I was enjoying the moment too. It was a good interview. I was talking to somebody that I had admired for 30 years and he knew that he was dealing with somebody who knew what he was talking about. He was loving it. He looked me straight in the eye, a glint of steel was still evident there, but his eyes were sparkling, even though he looked quite old to me – but then he had always looked old to me, even in his prime for City and England. As a player on the field, without his dentures, he looked like a swashbuckling Gabby Hayes, now he looked like everybody's favourite uncle, in his golf shirt and baggy sweater.

'If they wanted to play ... we could play; if they wanted it hard ... we could give it 'em hard. It didn't matter to us.'

I had asked a straight question and I had got an honest answer. It was not the answer that I had expected, but at least it was totally honest, even though it certainly did not mirror The Don's attitude to the game when he was a player.

Maybe we all recognize our own failings as footballers and, when given the opportunity to take charge of our own team, we try our best not to make the same mistakes twice, by encouraging the players to do the things that we could not do ourselves.

At Bradford, we went through a succession of managers, trainers and coaches as Park Avenue tried desperately and unsuccessfully to hang on to its league status until, eventually, the club's eccentric chairman, Herbert Metcalf, decided that he too would give us the benefit of his experience. One morning he travelled over the Pennines from his office in Manchester and, after the warm-up, he took over the session, still wearing his hat, waistcoat and business suit and told us that our set pieces were not quite what they should have been.

He lined up a defensive wall, stood with a polished brogue shoe on the muddy ball, turned to the players and asked: 'So, who's the best chipper?'

Every single player could have provided the answer, but we left it to our captain and spokesman, Graham Carr: 'Harry Ramsden!' he replied. 'People travel from everywhere, for six pennyworth and a fish.'

And from that moment the session was effectively over.

Even as a young player, the old trainers (coaches in those days were what transported the team to matches) used to single me out and hit me with their sage-like sayings and observations about the game, which I could not comprehend:

'Never trust a blond-haired full back.'

It took me nearly 25 years to work that one out.

'If you're getting no joy, then get some lime on yer boots.'

The Lilleshall coaching manual would probably say: 'If you, as an attacking central midfield player are finding the game a little difficult to adjust to, then try switching positions with a flank player.'

'You are the destroyers,' the trainer said, pointing to our bow-legged right back, our burly left back and our Desperate Dan look-alike centre half. 'You are the fetchers and carriers,' nodding to me, the two inside forwards and the left half. 'And you lot,' meaning the two little wingers and the centre forward, 'are the finisher-offers. OK?'

'OK,' we all replied in unison, and a couple of seconds later we were all out on the pitch. No problem.

Usually though, on match days, the trainer would sidle up to me in the dressing room about ten minutes before the game and give me the old smack on the thigh, which apparently covered just about everything

29

that he could not put into words. I never knew why they did that, but that was the bit that I used to look forward to the most!

Why me? I was no different to any other kid. I used to treat them with respect, which most of the other lads did not. But surely they deserved that. I used to listen and loved to hear their tales of the old days when, as they never tired of reminding me, 'players really were players'.

At Manchester City, our trainer Laurie Barnett, when he had remembered to switch on his hearing aid, used to chuckle about Roy Paul, the great Manchester City skipper.

Reserve trainer Fred Tilson just used to chuckle and try to pick a winner for the 2.30 at Sandown Park. Bill McGlen was forever reminiscing about Busby, Jack Rowley and Charlie Mitten's greyhounds: 'He used to put 'em under the heat lamp in the physio's room if they were racing that same evening, to get 'em nicely warmed up.' And the louder he laughed, the harder he dug his thumbs into your thigh.

Of Trevor Ford and Shackleton at Sunderland, Bill would say: 'Played one-twos off the corner flag Shack' did, and Fordy, he'd kick the balls off you – but what a gentleman he was. As soon as the game was over, he'd help you to look for them.

'And the ball, what about the ball? Inflation in our day, meant pumping 'em up! It weighed about a ton on a wet day, and Fordy would go around with "The sign of Zorro" on his forehead for days on end after a game, where he had connected with the lace.' More roars of laughter, and the thumbs would go in even deeper.

Then, of course, there was Milburn and Bobby Mitchell at Newcastle. 'J E T, those were his initials you know, John Edward Thompson Milburn. His parents must have known a thing or two to have christened him like that, because he was jet-propelled.

I know I would never have caught him when he was in full flight. Mind you, he couldn't limp very fast, so I always tried to give him one early on, Fred, you know what I mean.'

More laughter and more pain for me, as my injury became progressively worse, instead of better. What a smashing way to earn a living this is!

Name any great player from the past, and trainers like McGlen had either played with them, played against them, or most certainly could tell you a great story about them, and I loved to hear them all. In fact, I played against Bobby Mitchell myself, many years later, and, after all the stories McGlen had told me, I felt as if I had known him all my life and, I have to admit, that whenever I recall that game, I feel totally ashamed of myself.

Mitchell was a mercurial left winger for Newcastle United in the early 1950s when the FA Cup almost became their property and the Geordies seemed to monopolize Wembley Stadium. He was the mainspring behind nearly every Newcastle attack spanning about ten seasons and his magic invariably ended in goals for Milburn, George Robledo or Vic Keeble.

Newcastle United, of course, had beaten my team Manchester City 3–1 in the 1955 FA Cup final. I was 11 years old at the time, watching the game on our little black and white television set at home, and was absolutely inconsolable when right back Jimmy Meadows, four years later to become my coach at Manchester City, was carried from the field after twisting his knee while trying to cope with the trickery of Mitchell. So serious was the injury that not only was Meadows to take no further part in the game, but he was destined to take no further part in any game. His playing career was over from that moment, although he did make an abortive attempt at a comeback a few years later in a reserve game at Derby County. He played centre half, and borrowed my boots for the game ... so really he had no chance. Jim was fine, but my boots played their normal game.

It was Mitchell's fault of course, if he had been just an ordinary flying winger, Jim would not have twisted his knee, his blood, and just about everything else it is possible to twist, to try to cope with him. This is an 11-year-old with sky blue running through his veins speaking.

Still, all was not lost. Winger Bill Spurdle dropped back to mark Mitchell in the second half. He had played full back before, so I thought all would be well, because it was still only 1–1 at half time.

I have to confess that Spurdle was not one of my favourite players. He wore a dour, miserable expression, and hailed from the Channel Islands, so I was suspicious of him: because I did not know where the Channel Islands were. Spurs centre forward Len Duquemin was from there as well, and I always kept a wary eye on him for the same reason. I now know their location and realize how beautiful and tax-free they are, so Matthew Le Tissier and Graeme Le Saux have nothing to fear. I like them – but I would not have done in 1955!

At this point, however, my hopes and dreams of seeing Manchester City win the FA Cup rested fairly and squarely on the shoulders of this Channel Islander. My boy Bill, I am sad to recall, found the wing wizard simply too much for him to comprehend and Mitchell himself did not help matters by constantly coming deep into the hole that had been left on the right-hand side, where Spurdle should have been playing prior to the reshuffle, and demanding and receiving a stream of pin-point cross-field passes from the feet of Jimmy Scoular, the thunder-thighed Scotsman wearing the Number 4 jersey for Newcastle.

Mitchell then began to weave his magic by shuffling

up to Spurdle with oceans of room in which to manoeuvre, and proceeded to glide and slide past him almost at will – inside, outside, over, under, through his legs, backwards – you name it, he seemed to be doing it, while I was left to squirm helplessly in anguish on the settee. The unbearable heat, the famous stamina-sapping Wembley turf, 10 men playing against 11, Mitchell torturing the life out of my heroes – it was all too much, and inevitably the game ended in a 3–1 victory for The Magpies. I was not a happy boy as I watched Jimmy Scoular receive the FA Cup from the Queen and he was then hoisted triumphantly, high onto the shoulders of team-mates Bob Stokoe and ... Bobby Mitchell!

A lot of water had flowed along the River Tyne since that day. It was Redheugh Park instead of St James' Park, the North Regional League not the Football League, but all the tell-tale features were still in evidence, as I watched the opposition shooting in before the game. The hair was still wavy, although there was not now quite as much of it, he was a little heavier around the thighs and girth, but the left foot was as sweet as a nut as he fired shots at his goalkeeper, who looked young enough to be his son.

Yes, it was him alright! I could only see him from the back, still wearing the familiar Number 11, even though he was now wearing the white shirt of Gateshead and not the famous black and white stripes of Newcastle United. The style and grace were unmistakable. I could not imagine how old he was, but it was definitely Bobby Mitchell. I was mesmerized. I was back at Wembley. There he was, dancing and prancing his way along the touchline, crossing endless balls into City's overworked penalty area ... the sound of the referee's whistle brought me back to earth, back to the equally down-to-earth surroundings of Gateshead Football Club.

Centre forward Frank McKenna rolled the ball the customary couple of yards to his inside left, Steele, who in one movement swept the ball out to Mitchell wide on the left touchline. I had lined up about 50 yards away in the left half position, but startled everybody by sprinting (that in itself was a shock!) across the entire width of the pitch and, before Bobby Mitchell could get into his third shuffling stride, I had hit him with the most horrendous tackle that it has ever been my misfortune to perpetrate.

I can remember the mixture of old age, horror, shock and downright disbelief on his face as I clattered into him and left him in a tangled heap on the floor. His pension book flew out of his back pocket, outraged officials leaped from the bench, my own manager buried his head in his hands. And, as I stood over him, the red mist began to clear from my eyes.

It has to be said that Bobby Mitchell, lying in a crumpled heap at my feet was, as well as being a truly great player, also a gentleman footballer, who in a matter of seconds had managed to regain both his composure and his dignity. Instead of reacting equally violently, as he was fully entitled to do, he looked up at me like a homeless bloodhound, blinked his doleful eyes, with bags under them like John Wayne's saddlebags and, with a light Scottish lilt in his voice, gently asked: 'What was that for?'

By now my head had cleared completely; I was again that nice lad with good manners from Crosslee School. As I surveyed the wreckage, I felt a mixture of stupidity and inadequacy as I mumbled: 'Dunno. For 1955, I suppose.'

He looked at me as if I were the village idiot, somebody to be pitied, sighed a little and held out his hand for me to help him shakily to his feet. His action probably saved me from the indignity of the quickest sending off on record. We then tried to get on with the game.

That sort of thing had happened to me only once before, when I found myself playing against Bobby Johnstone at Oldham Athletic. Bobby was a fantastic footballer, who was bought by City from Hibernian, supposedly to replace Don Revie, who was having another dispute with the club. I went to see Johnstone's first appearance in a pre-season game at Maine Road, Blues against Maroons, first team against the reserves, and I could not believe his skill. In fact, after he had scored past reserve keeper John Savage, the big man turned to us all standing behind the goals and said it was the best goal he had ever seen, let alone had scored against him.

I was still only ten years old, but I could tell that Johnstone was something special. He was a Scottish international, born in Selkirk and had been one of the Hibs Famous Five – Gordon Smith, Bobby Johnstone, Lawrie Reilly, Eddie Turnbull and Willie Ormond – who were the stars of the Scottish football league. He was brilliant during his spell at Maine Road. A little portly and reported to like a drink or three, he nevertheless produced the goods on the field where it matters and scored a goal in each of City's FA Cup final appearances.

Eventually he moved along the road to Oldham Athletic where he, more than anyone, helped to re-vitalize an ailing club and put them onto the football map, long before Joe Royle came along to finish the job off.

By the time I came into contact with him, Bobby was playing the game by memory but, unfortunately for me, he did not suffer from amnesia this day at Boundary Park, where he proceeded to play round me as if I was not there. I had watched him play for so long from the terraces that I was finding it difficult to break the habit and I was now enjoying watching him perform from close quarters.

Bobby Johnstone never broke sweat during that first 45 minutes and, if he did, I could not detect the aroma of Tetley's best bitter. His passing was like radar, as he ambled about the midfield like Robert Morley in a blue and white halved jersey. In fact, those quaint Oldham shirts of the day were probably the only halves that Bobby Johnstone ever had! It was 3–0 at half time, Johnstone had scored two and laid on the other one and, generally speaking, I thought that it had been a good game to watch! I trooped into the dressing room with the rest of the lads for the usual cuppa and a bollocking.

The dressing-room door closed behind the last man in and all was strangely quiet, but everybody seemed to be staring in my direction. It was obvious what they were thinking so, being a bright, quick-thinking Blackley lad, I decided that, unlike the previous 45 minutes, attack was definitely the best form of defence.

'Don't all look at me,' I protested. 'I was nowhere near him when he scored his two goals!'

As soon as I had uttered the words, I realized that I had not quite got it right.

'Precisely,' I was told in no uncertain terms. 'Is there any possible chance that you might get somewhere near to him during the next 45 minutes?'

Johnstone was a great player to watch, though. Albert Quixall was Oldham's other inside forward ... I enjoyed watching him that day too!

CHAPTER 4

A place in the sun

Goalkeeper Bob Ward, then of Wigan Athletic, now the much-respected physiotherapist of first division Chelsea (where he puts his fingertips to much better use!), looked across a sea of empty San Miguel bottles tottering precariously on a little bar table by the beach in Magaluf, paused for effect, shielded his eyes from the blazing sun, gave me a knowing little smile and said quite seriously for a second: 'You know Fred, as far as you are concerned, I reckon if it was a straight choice between half an hour with Joan Collins and half an hour talking football with Bobby Moore, Joan Collins wouldn't even get into the frame.'

It was the close-season break. It had been a good campaign for Wigan, the football league's newest team, we had finished a creditable sixth, not bad considering our somewhat dicky start. The chairman and directors were showing their appreciation to the players and staff by sending us for a week in Majorca, where we could all lie on the sand and look at the stars, although the players would have preferred Malibu Beach near Hollywood, where they fancied their chances of lying on the stars and looking at the sand!! But that's foot-ballers for you – ever the optimists!

We could have been the Barclays of bottle banks that particular lunchtime, as half the Wigan playing staff, my coach Brooky and I put the football world to rights. I was glad that Brooky was with us that day. He is my great friend and confidant, a former playing colleague who for years had suffered from barphobia – the fear of buying a drink – now here he was in full swig with the rest of us.

We solved manager Ian McNeill's problems for him and generally slagged off any unfortunate player or official who happened not to be with us at that moment. We picked the best-ever Wigan team ... I wasn't in it! We went on to choose the best Manchester City team of all time ... I was not in that one either, Colin Bell beat me by the odd vote! The best England team ... no chance there, although I fancied myself for the Republic of Ireland team, because I am a good friend of Frank Stapleton and I once shook hands with a milkman from Taplow who delivers Terry Wogan's milk every morning. Better qualifications than most of the Republic's players, I felt, but I did not get in their team either – I cannot kick the ball high enough!

We discussed the merits of Law and Best. Who was the greatest, Matthews or Finney? And who had the edge: my all-time favourite Bobby Moore or Willie Young? I was in my element. Surrounded by footballers, talking about football past and present. I could not imagine a better way to spend a day, hence Wardy's penetrating observation, regarding the delectable Miss Collins.

The ideal solution to this conundrum, of course, would be three minutes with Joan Collins and the remaining 27 talking football with Bobby. But when the lads pushed me for a direct answer, I had to leave membership of the Joan Collins Fan Club to Julian Clary. After all, the former England captain has managed 45 minutes each way with some of the best players in the world – not even the lovely Joan Collins could compete with that, could she?

38

It was not a unanimous decision, of course. In fact, I lost 8–1. Are you listening Mrs Brooks? But they all agreed that I certainly talked a good game, no matter who I might be discussing it with. To a man they were certain that I would most definitely have been doing Miss Collins a big favour by giving her a body swerve, in view of my past record with beautiful, famous, female movie stars. And they never wasted an opportunity of reminding me of the occasion.

A couple of seasons prior to the trip to Majorca, while I was still a player, albeit an ageing one, but one who was still capable of grabbing the Number 3 shirt before anybody else could get their grubby little hands on it, I was a member of a squad that toured America playing half a dozen games in some of the major towns and cities. After our game in Los Angeles, I had arranged to meet my pal, singing star Malcolm Roberts, who had invited me to stay with him for a few days. Malcolm, an old schoolfriend of mine from Blackley, had enjoyed considerable success in England with his good looks and powerful singing voice and, after hitting the charts with a couple of singles, had decided to try his luck in America, following the success of Tom Jones and Englebert Humperdinck.

He met me at the Beverly Hilton Hotel – where else? And, before jet-lag and post-match *rigor mortis* could set in, he whisked me off to a party at the house of one of America's most famous sultry female singers. It was my first visit to the capital of Cardboard California, so I was not yet used to being surrounded by gleaming teeth, with everyone hoping that I 'have a nice day' when really they couldn't give a toss. Nor was I used to being served breakfast or coffee every time I took my seat in a coffee shop by an aspiring actor who had just sent his ten-by-eight glossies off to the William Morris Agency.

Still, I had no worries; I was with my old mate. Malc

would look after me. He seemed to have adjusted to his new lifestyle very easily. His flowing mane had been bleached by the sun. His snow-white trousers looked as though they had been sprayed on, while his flowered shirt, with the correct number of buttons left undone, revealed a discreet little medallion the size of a digestive biscuit. His shirt collar, of course, was in the upright position à la Billy Fury 1961. He had an even tan and molars which, while not the genuine Hollywood reconstruction job, were certainly in better shape than when he used to go to that little National Health dentist near Crumpsall Hospital. Provided he did not fall off his white, patent-leather Cuban-heeled boots, he would be OK, and I felt very comfortable alongside him in my little short-sleeved shirt that my Mother had got for me from Conran Street market and my grey slacks with matching shoes from Freeman, Hardy and Willis.

Two carboys came to park our car: 'I've forgotten how to put a car into reverse since I came here,' Malc confessed, as we rang the bell.

'Darling!' The door was opened by a set of teeth.

'This is my mate Fred from England,' Malcolm announced.

'Darling,' the teeth said to me, while gazing over my shoulder to see if anybody really worth knowing was following behind. In we went, and that was the last I saw of Malcolm until it was time to go home.

I found a little corner for myself and proceeded to watch the world go by. The jet-lag still eluded me. Various concoctions were put into my hand, and beautiful people drifted by. Many sets of pearlies were flashed in my direction, as various visions passed before my eyes, both male and female, but nobody stopped to utter a word to me. Nobody even hoped I'd 'have a nice day'. Actually, I felt quite content; I was mildly amused by the antics of those around me, and I was quietly enjoying my little self, seeing how the other half lived, and quite relieved that I would only be part of it for about five or six hours before returning to the real world, when this lovely young lady obviously decided that I had been sitting on my own for long enough.

Being a gentleman, and a well brought-up Blackley boy into the bargain, I struggled to my feet as she approached and this show of typically olde English good manners cost me a searing pain in my right knee, as two cartilages clicked like castanets in the Edmundo Ros Orchestra. She was obviously a good-hearted young thing and felt sorry for this poor old sod sitting on his own in the corner, and I gave her full marks for making the effort.

I thought that she was possibly training for a job with the Samaritans, so I went along with it as she struggled to find a bit of common ground, so that after a suitable length of time she would be able to go off and mingle with the rest of the crowd, comforted by the knowledge that she had done her good deed for the day. We agreed that we were indeed both from England, I could tell that by her beautifully educated accent, and I am sure that she had already guessed the same before I had even opened my mouth by my braces, the hand-kerchief knotted in each corner on my head and the copy of *Charles Buchan's Football Monthly* jutting out of my back pocket. She seemed a bright girl!

'I really like your trousers,' she said, pointing to the designer C&A label on the waistband.

I had to give the girl credit, she was doing her best. There we were, surrounded by athletic young actors and slim male models parading in gear freshly bought and tailored on Rodeo Drive that very morning, and she was admiring a pair of creased gabardine slacks bought from C&A.

'Yes! An exclusive little boutique on Carrisbrook

Street, Claude & André, they make them for me, you know,' I replied.

'In Chelsea?'

'No! Between Harpurhey and Collyhurst.'

But by then she had made her big mistake: she had mentioned the name of a football team. Any team would have suited me, but I was quite happy with Chelsea, and we spent the next half-hour discussing Stamford Bridge, Peter Osgood, Charlie Cooke, Peter Bonetti and I even threw in Roy Bentley and Eric Parsons from the 1950s for good measure.

What a game girl!

She tried her best to look interested as I rattled on. She may not have done before, but she sure knew the difference between 4–2–4 and 4–3–3 from that moment. She kept nodding (off!) in most of the correct places, constantly stroking her hair with one hand, while stifling a yawn with the other.

Her hair was her most striking feature, even *I* noticed her hair. It flowed all the way down her back. She had a beautiful oval-shaped face, lovely skin, big eyes, a voice like velvet and perfect teeth that looked natural, unlike their Californian counterparts. In fact, she looked like a film star. But film stars are too wrapped up in themselves to feel sorry for some geezer from England whose mate has left him on his own in a strange house, in a strange country, 3,000 miles from home. Film stars are not that considerate, they only talk about themselves, don't they?

I think it was when I was discussing the far-post crosses of Frank Blunstone and the goalscoring instincts of Bobby Tambling that she decided that she had done her bit for England and she moved effortlessly away in search of some food.

Malcolm then decided to renew his acquaintance with me. 'You and Jane seemed to be getting along very well, was she telling you how much she misses England?'

'Is that her name?' I replied. 'I was just educating her about the history of Chelsea Football Club.'

Malcolm, obviously despairing of me, decided it was time to go.

I will say this though: if Jane Seymour ever becomes fed up playing sexy James Bond girls on the silver screen, or Wallis Simpson, Marie Antoinette or Maria Callas in mini-blockbusters on our TV screens, she could always get a job as a social worker, hospital visitor, or any similar job that requires kindness and patience. Or, for that matter, she could even become the official statistician for Chelsea Football Club – she certainly knows enough about it now.

CHAPTER 5

The world loves a trier

Things were quite definitely looking up for me now: quiet little tête-à-têtes with famous film stars, touring America playing football while my business interests prospered back home. I began to feel that life, at last, was dealing me a good hand. It had not always been so, at various stages of my young playing life; I had been discarded by my favourite team Manchester City at the age of 19 at a time when I was really not fit enough to go anywhere else. I had been ostracized at Lincoln City, written off as a physical wreck at Huddersfield Town, freed by Crewe Alexandra and half a dozen other clubs, released by Bradford Park Avenue. And so it went on, until my body and ego were both covered in bruises, where managers *had* touched me with a ten-foot barge pole.

In retrospect, the setbacks I received in my early days were quite horrendous; indeed, looking back, I cannot imagine how or why I kept coming back for more punishment. Don't let anybody ever tell you that I do not love the game, or that I did not give it every single drop of sweat that I had to give. I gave it everything. Indeed, to illustrate the point, I still have, as one of my most treasured possessions, a programme from many years ago where, as usual, the pen pictures of the visitors is a main feature. It contained all the usual

44

biographical details, with about an inch of space allocated to each player including his vital statistics, career details and clubs to date.

Goalkeeper: A paragraph about him.
Right back: Kevin Connor – Signed from Rochdale, a little on the small side for a full back, but makes up for his lack of inches with his speed and tenacious tackling.
Left back: Peter Jones – A former Busby Babe with Manchester United, he made one league appearance for them before moving to the Racecourse Ground where he made 226 appearances for Wrexham. A very experienced defender equally at home at centre half or at full back.

And so it went on – right half, centre half – until it got to me and it said simply:

Left half: Fred Eyre – A trier.

That was all it said. End of story.

I think that when the day comes, the day when the referee blows my final whistle and I go to the great penalty area in the sky, I will instruct David Kilpatrick, monumental stonemason to the stars, that I will have those two words engraved on my tombstone. It just about sums the whole job up. For Vinny Jones, Wimbledon's favourite son, if I placed his order the inscription would read: 'WHO ARE YOU LOOKING AT??'

Initially, I had also struggled to find a job outside football. I left school on Friday with no qualifications other than a pair of twinkling feet and started as a young footballer with Manchester City three days later. Now, here I was, the owner of a highly successful stationery business and still involved in my real love –

football – as a member of the coaching staff at Wigan Athletic. Amazingly, I had also become the author of an autobiography, that for some reason had captured the imagination.

'Things look swell, things look great, I could have the whole world on a plate.' Maybe I could have become a songwriter as well!

I remember listening, many years ago, to Tommy Steele, a performer that I have always loved, saying that he believed that sooner or later every person is dealt a good hand at least once in their lifetime, but in most cases that person fails to recognize the fact. They then play their cards wrongly, so their big chance passes them by without them even knowing it. I remember thinking at the time that this was indeed a very profound observation, and one which I felt was probably right. So, with this in mind, I intended to make sure that I would be the one who played my cards very close to my chest.

One of the bonuses from the success of *Kicked into Touch* is the personal satisfaction I feel whenever I receive letters from people from all over the world, from different walks of life, telling me how much they have enjoyed the book, each one seemingly for a different individual reason. I must, however, admit to a feeling of extra pleasure when just occasionally a letter pops through my door and it is from somebody that I have admired for many years.

As a youngster, I was brought up watching the early American films and TV shows: *Sabu the Elephant Boy* – he is 86 now and even the elephants have forgotten him – and *Flash Gordon* of course, he must be about the same age – they just call him Gordon nowadays. Then there were the comedy shows like *Amos 'n' Andy, Bilko, I Love Lucy* and *The Burns and Allen Show,* in the days when the whole world loved the delicate but dizzy Gracie Allen, and George Burns made standing next to her, puffing on his cigar and asking, 'Gracie, how's your brother?' an art form. Sadly Gracie died in 1964, but George, a vaudevillian trouper to the tip of his cigar, kept going – a fellow trier you see! – and carved out another career for himself as a famous film star, with an Oscar-winning performance alongside Walter Matthau as one of *The Sunshine Boys* and followed this by playing the part of God in his next movie. Until they make the life story of Jimmy Hill, you cannot get any higher than that!

The envelope was light green, the name and address said simply 'Fred Eyre, Author, Manchester, England', but it had still found me. They are marvellous, the GPO: they now have high-powered machines that can sort a million letters a minute ... then they give them to a bloke on a bicycle to deliver! Still, they had done their stuff this time.

The writing was a little spidery. The address on the flap read 'Hillcrest Country Club, Beverly Hills, Los Angeles'. I thought it must be from Malcolm Roberts as I slit open the envelope. He was the only person I knew in LA – Hillcrest Country Club? – he must be moving up in the world. And it was typical of him to forget my address.

A coloured postcard slipped out. It was a picture of the great George Burns, complete with cigar, of course, and on the back he had written:

To Fred
Hope this eventually finds you.
Stay happy and healthy kid and
keep writing those great books.
Best wishes
    George Burns

I stared at it for ages, propped it up against the milk jug on the breakfast table, and stared at it some more. I could not believe that George Burns, a great artist, famous the world over, almost 90 years of age at the time, could possibly have felt moved enough to sit down and take the trouble to write to me from the other side of the world. I would not even have thought that Natty – that's what his really close friends call him and, of course, I now include myself among the select band – would know anything about the English variety of football, but who cares? Besides, I have had letters from directors of football clubs who know even less about the game than Natty!

Somebody who does know a little about the game, especially his first love Crystal Palace, is Roy Hudd. I never miss *The News Hudd Lines* whenever I am travelling to a game somewhere. I always tune in to listen to Roy's wonderful originality and wit at Saturday lunchtimes. He is such an authority on Olde Tyme Music Hall, and the great entertainers of that era, that I could listen to his anecdotes for hours. It was a marvellous feeling for me to receive a couple of letters from Roy extolling the virtues of *Kicked into Touch*, and also to receive a little note from Tommy Steele, another favourite of mine, congratulating me on its success.

These are people who have reached the very top of their professions, who have taken a few minutes to scribble a few lines to me, somebody that they do not know or even need to know. They were little gestures that I will never forget, and never could I have imagined, years ago, as I watched *The Burns and Allen Show*, or bought my first-ever record, 'Singing the Blues' by Tommy Steele. Not long afterwards I received the first of my annual free transfers. That is a letter of a different kind, one guaranteed to plunge any young footballer on the receiving end into the very depths of despair.

It was a feeling that I came to know very well

indeed. So my advice to any young kid in the same position is: it's not where you start, but where you finish – and I am going to finish on top.

That's two songs I have written in one chapter ... I think I will send this one to Bonnie Langford to see if she likes it.

CHAPTER 6

I'm free!

What do Lee Dixon, Gary Bennett, Dean Saunders, Ray Houghton, David Platt and Mickey Quinn all have in common? They, together with many more great players, were given free transfers as youngsters before their careers had really got off the ground. I am something of an expert when it comes to free transfers, having received 20 of them in my time! So I reckon that I know what I am talking about.

Nowadays, of course, older players are sometimes awarded free transfers as a thanks for services rendered. This magnanimous gesture by the club, of waiving a prospective fee, enables the player to negotiate a fat signing-on fee for himself from his new club, which, of course, is a situation that he finds quite acceptable. Indeed, some are more than prepared to do battle with the board of directors in order to obtain one, but, while the name is still the same, I can assure you that to be given a free transfer at the age of 18 is a completely different proposition.

At the stroke of a pen or, quite often in my case, the opening of a newspaper, the prospect of a glittering career as a professional footballer is, from that moment, over, unless the manager from another club comes along to offer you a second chance. Your legs, quite literally, have been chopped from underneath you, as clinically as a Norman Whiteside tackle.

Obviously, the first feeling on receiving the news is one of deep hurt. How could anybody possibly think that I am not good enough for this team? But it is only one man's opinion that has brought this about and even the greatest managers, the finest judges of talent, have been known to make a mistake. Mind you, in my case, I don't really think that 20 of them could have been wrong!

Arsenal's Lee Dixon is now one of the top attacking right backs in the country – a swift, pacy player, with a league championship medal in his back pocket and England caps sitting proudly on the sideboard of his parents' home in Winsford. Lee, whose father, Roy, was a goalkeeper at Manchester City just before my time at Maine Road, was given a free transfer at the age of 18 by John Bond, at that time the manager of Burnley.

Gary Bennett, Sunderland's captain in their triumphant return to the first division, was also given a free transfer in 1981 at the age of 18 by Manchester City, who were managed at the time by John Bond.

Dean Saunders, the flying little striker from Wales, who was transferred from Oxford United to Derby County for a massive £1,000,000, was given a free transfer as a kid from Swansea. And their manager was ... John Bond!

If only John had been a manager during my playing career, you would not be able to move in my house now for England caps!

Ray Houghton and David Platt, however, managed to hit the big time without 'Bondy's' assistance. Houghton was freed by West Ham United and, after putting his career back together at Fulham and Oxford, he finally went into orbit at Liverpool, with a big money move to Anfield.

Platt, meanwhile, was forced to exchange the luxury of life at Manchester United for the railway sidings of Crewe. No money changed hands then, but £200,000 found its way into the Crewe coffers when David moved on to Aston Villa and now, of course, he is priceless. His World Cup goals for England have made him one of the biggest names in football.

In terms of actual money, however, my own Mickey Quinn could quite easily top the lot. Quinn was one of my young players and, from the age of 16, I loved everything about the lad. I loved his attitude, I loved the way he would beg me for extra shooting practice after normal training every Friday morning. I loved his temperament: 'Chances during a game are just like buses ... you miss one, but sooner or later another one comes along.' I loved his big floppy feet, that seemed to have a mind of their own and went through a pair of Puma S.P.A. King almost every six weeks; and most of all, I loved the fact that he scored goals with them almost every week, with monotonous regularity. He was only a kid, but he did a man-sized job for me at Wigan; and though he was a bit of a scallywag, he had a heart of gold the size of a lion and would run through brick walls for you.

He comes from the Cantrill Farm area of Liverpool. A lion once escaped from nearby Knowsley Safari Park, drifted into the area, and was severely mauled by Quinny's mates!

He used to run his own mobile disco in the evenings, a practice frowned upon by the directors, who thought that it was not quite the right image for a young professional footballer. They were right of course, but I decided to turn a blind eye to the situation. Knowing the type of lad he was, I thought it would do him no harm to keep the thing going, because he enjoyed it so much. Indeed, it saved me from giving him many a bollocking, because, if ever he had a poor first half, all that was needed at half time was a slow shake of my head, a pitying look and 'Don't you ever sell that disco ... you're going to need it if you carry on like this.'

52

Nothing else needed to be said. One night Quinny was on his way home from a gig, trundling his gear through Canny Farm when a policeman approached him and said: 'Excuse me, sir! Would you mind accompanying me to the police station.'

Michael protested his innocence in the only way he knew how: 'Yer wot? I haven't done nottin!'

'I know that, sir,' the constable replied. 'But I'm too frightened to walk there by myself!'

For a young lad, Mick Quinn featured quite prominently in my days at Wigan. We took him on a pre-season tour of the West Country, manager Larry Lloyd's home territory, and played games against Bristol Rovers, Yeovil and Frome Town among others, and after Quinn had scored every single goal that the club scored on the trip, about 12 or 13 in all, Larry told Mike Langley of the *Sunday People* that he would not sell Mickey Quinn for half a million ... a colossal amount in those days, especially for a young kid. And, do you know what? Larry was right, because not long after, another club was eventually given £2,000 to take the lad away for nothing.

By that time, I had long since departed. Quinn would have been allowed to leave over my dead body – although I am sure that Larry would have been more than delighted to have arranged that!

I was in my shop in Manchester when the telephone rang and I recognized the dulcet tones of Eric Webster, enquiring about the merits of young Quinn. I had known Eric for years. He had been one of the shrewdest operators in non-league football when I was a player – so shrewd in fact, that he was one of the few who did not sign me! And he was now manager of nearby Stockport County.

I duly extolled the virtues of the player, but put a little dampener on things at the end by adding 'but with all due respect to your club, Eric, I think he would be a little out of your price bracket.'

'How does two grand sound to you?' replied Eric.

'Two grand for Mickey Quinn, they must be joking. Get in your car, drive over there and sign him before they increase the price.'

'No Fred, you don't understand,' Eric was obviously enjoying himself now. 'They are offering us £2,000 to take the lad off their hands.'

So the best young centre forward in the country went to Stockport County, with £2,000 thrown in for good measure, and was eventually sold to Oldham for a healthy profit. From there he went to Portsmouth for triple the price and, over 50 goals later, he joined the exclusive set of Number 9s who became legends of St James' Park by scoring over 30 goals in one season for Newcastle United. He was one of The Magpies' most expensive signings at £680,000, but they are now knocking back bids in excess of £1,000,000 to hang on to him.

The fragrance of success smells just that bit sweeter when you know that the player lording it at the top of goalscoring charts is someone like Quinn; or that the lad picking up the championship medal is like Dixon; or that the one galloping up the steps to the Royal Box to be presented with an FA Cup-winners' medal is a boy like Wimbledon's Terry Phelan. He was once, as a pair, 'freed', together with his young full-back partner Dennis Irwin, by Leeds United.

Irwin later joined Manchester United for a mammoth fee and is now a fully fledged Irish international, so it's lovely to remember that these same star players, in their early, learning days, were kicked so hard in the goolies by the opinion of one so-called expert that they thought that their careers were over before they had even started. But they 'picked themselves up, dusted themselves off and started all over again'.

I reckon that could be song number three!

CHAPTER 7

Keys to Wembley

'Hey! young man. Now don't mess me about. Do you want to play for me or not?' It was the unmistakable voice of Brian Clough on the other end of the line.

The nasal tone, all the inflections were there, the traces of his Teesside childhood still very much in evidence. The emphasis so easily recognizable in the words 'young' and the lingering 't' on the end of the word 'not' ... but it did not fool me for a second.

'Hello Richard,' I replied. 'What's Anne Diamond been up to now?'

I was so used to receiving such phone calls from Richard Keys that they had almost become a way of life in the Eyre household and, indeed, I would know that there was something seriously wrong if ever he felt the need to call me using the voice that the ladies loved to wake up to every morning on TV-AM.

Richard, I am pleased to say, had made a big name for himself as one of the anchor persons – can you believe it? I'll be from Personchester before long, I'm sure! – on TV-AM, with his good looks, charm, urbanity and the hairiest arms seen on television since Desmond Morris presented *Zootime.* So much so that for the first month viewers were convinced that he was wearing the same long-sleeved angora sweater every morning ... they did not realize that they were looking at his arms!

Richard Keys had done me many great favours in my life but, by making this telephone call, he was doing the biggest favour he could possibly do for an old man who still loved football and who still thought he could play a bit, albeit only a teeny weeny bit! (Some things never change, and my optimism is one of them.)

'Do you want to play at Wembley?' he enquired, now reverting to his normal well-modulated tones.

'Is the Pope a Catholic?' I replied without a trace of excitement in my voice. That is how ridiculous I thought the question was.

'Well, do you or don't you?' he repeated, and my tiny, 42-year-old ticker skipped a little beat as I detected a hint of seriousness in his voice.

I decided there and then on the subtle, don't-seem-too-anxious-I'll-check-my-diary approach.

'YES!' I blurted out, before he had had time to finish his sentence.

'It's a serious game, no messing about, all great players, for half an hour before the Freight Rover Trophy Final, Bristol City v Bolton Wanderers. What position do you want to play?'

This sounded too good to be true. Not only was I being offered the opportunity to tread the hallowed turf at last, but I could choose my own position as well. Again I tried not to sound too overcome. I was tempted to say that I would play at centre forward. After all, I was considered at my peak to be the finest finisher since Jim Peters! But I decided that discretion was the better part of valour.

'Anywhere in the back four will do me nicely, boss,' I replied, immediately slipping back into the creeping vernacular that for 20 years had been a feature of my playing career.

'That's OK then,' my new manager (the 30th of my career!) went on. 'But you can't wear the Number 6 jersey.'

This seemed like the usual story: I was not the first choice after all, and was not slow in feigning my annoyance at being told that one of the back four positions had already been filled.

'Bobby Moore is wearing Number 6.'

This was just too much for me to take in. I was beginning to feel one of my headaches coming on with excitement. Not only was I to play at Wembley, but I would have Bobby Moore alongside me in the back four. I am unashamedly Bobby Moore's number one fan, he is my all-time favourite footballer by a mile and the thought of passing him in the street, let alone passing him the ball, was enough to make me feel like an 18-year-old again – but it is difficult to get one at my age!

'Fair enough, gaffer,' I replied. 'I'll play left back and try to help him through the game!'

'Gaffer' is the name that players use these days when referring to the manager and, just because I still used dubbin on my boots and sucked Dextrosol tablets before the game, I did not want him to start thinking that I was a bit too long in the dentures for the job in hand.

With the names Eyre and Moore firmly entrenched in the back four, I really could not give a toss who the other eight members of the team would be. I rightly assumed that Richard himself would undertake the role of player/manager ... I mean player/gaffer – old habits die hard. (What do they use instead of dubbin? I must treat myself to a tin.) He then proceeded to rattle off the team and I was the only player in it that I did not know!

As well as England's World Cup-winning captain alongside me at the back, I would have Tony Currie just in front of me in midfield, with George Best completing a nice little triangle at outside left ... if I cannot play well surrounded by that little lot, then I really am the bad player that everybody says I am!

'Well, thanks a lot, Rich,' I concluded. 'If there's anything I can do to repay you for this, just let me know, a trip round the world on Concorde, a yacht in Marbella, my right arm ... just name it, mate. What? We're playing a Football League XI selected by Football League secretary Graham Kelly? That's fine Richard.' (No need for the grovelling gaffer business now that I am in the team!)

I could not have cared less if it was Real Madrid we were playing, with Puskas and di Stefano, I was going to play at Wembley and that was all that I was interested in. But nevertheless, as I lay back on my bed to take in the situation, I thought to myself that Graham Kelly would have the pick of a lot of top-quality players, so I had better do a bit of training ... only a bit though. I did not want to peak early!

Richard's phone call had delayed me somewhat. That, plus the fact that I had telephoned everybody that I had met during the last 25 years to tell them the news, meant that I was a little late getting into the shop that morning and the next couple of hours were spent trying to catch up with myself and to keep my mind off the twin towers, until another phone call interrupted things again.

'Can I speak to Mr Fred Eyre please?' the lady's sweet voice chirped out.

'Speaking,' I replied, holding the phone between my left ear and left shoulder as I tried to do four jobs at once.

'Mr Graham Kelly for you, the Football League,' she said, putting me through.

'Fred, how would you like to play for my team at Wembley?'

I could not believe this. I had waited 42 years and never got within a sniff of wintergreen of the place; the ball had never even been hit into the crowd within 70 yards of me (even when Willie Young was playing!), and now in the space of two hours, I had been asked to play for both sides.

'Graham,' I stammered. 'I don't know how to say this, I'm really flattered, but I'm playing for the other team.'

I could hardly believe it was my voice that I was hearing saying such a thing. Graham, to his credit, at least sounded disappointed. He was probably punching the air with delight at the other end of the telephone ... but what could I do? It had to be the MBE – Moore, Best and Eyre!!

CHAPTER 8

Moore, Best, Charlton and King John

I am delighted to say that I was not disappointed with Mr Robert Frederick Moore. I had such a high regard for him as a player that I desperately wanted him to be a nice person as well. Sadly, there have been so many instances over the years where seemingly funny, warm and much-loved entertainers, usually comedians or actors, have proved to be, in reality, miserable, rude and sometimes downright nasty individuals when you actually meet them.

It would not have been the end of the world for me, of course, if Bobby Moore had been like that, but I would have felt very deflated ... it would be a bit like being told that Nanette Newman does not actually do the washing up! Indeed, one or two of my pals in the game, players who used to train with him every day at West Ham, like goalkeeper Peter Grotier, striker Brian Dear and Bournemouth manager Harry Redknapp, had discussed Bobby with me from time to time over the years at my instigation of course, and each one of them had said what a smashing bloke he is. So I thought that if those three great characters had given him the thumbs up, then there would be no problem.

So, there we all were in the dressing room, ten

minutes before we were due onto the pitch, and the only player not in evidence so far was Mr Moore – even George Best had turned up. Since George had joined AA with his drink problem, it meant that he could still get drunk, but they would get him to his destination! He was quietly preparing himself for the game: no fuss, just sipping a soft drink from a can and quickly slipping into his gear; a word here, a smile there, he always seems such a nice lad. I really like George Best.

As with most controversial stars, there are horrendous stories circulating about George Best, possibly some are true, but I can only speak how I find, and George has always been a first-class fellow as far as I am concerned. He has turned up every single time I have ever been due to meet him or appear with him, he has always been polite and obliging to people. As well as the 500 top-class games in which he has played, he must have turned out in almost as many for charity to raise money for countless causes and ex-players up and down the country. He may not have done himself any favours with his appearance on *Wogan*, but that was not the George Best that I know, I am very glad to say.

I first met him when he was 16 years of age, playing for Manchester United in the 'B' team. At that time I was still at Manchester City and, obviously, I did not know then that he was going to develop into one of the world's all-time great players. The sad thing is that he retired too early and deprived the public of watching him play for a few more years. Sad also for George, because, like all great players, he just loves to play.

Frank Worthington, for all his playboy image, liked nothing better than to be out on the field, either playing or training, simply because he loved to play. I have known him since he was 15 years of age. He comes from a footballing family steeped in the game and he loves it now as much as he always did.

Similarly, at Queen's Park Rangers it is no secret

61

that Stan Bowles spent plenty of time in the bookies, but he would always be the one to stay behind after training, having a bit of fun, showing his great skill to the young apprentices, because he just loved it. If only he could have passed the betting shop the way he passed the ball. And it was the same with George: he loved to play the game, he did not need a capacity crowd, just a ball – and then he would be happy.

I went along to training one glorious sunny morning at the Hollywood Racetrack in Los Angeles. George had defected to the States and was then playing for The Aztecs, who used this famous, massive racetrack for training most days. It was deserted, except for the players going through their paces in the hot sunshine, waiting for the inevitable little six-a-side game at the end of the session. George did his running just like the rest of the lads, although a little within himself I thought. But when they started playing with a ball, he was dribbling, running, chasing, laughing, falling over, scoring goals, missing goals, just like a ten-year-old kid.

'A minute to go in the Cup final,' he screamed, like any excited youngster in any park in the world would, as the cross came over and he threw himself at it for a diving header. There were no adoring fans in sight out there in the middle of the deserted racetrack, nobody to impress – but he was having great fun.

He may well have decided to quit because of outside pressures, things not really connected to the game, but I have seen enough to know, and it certainly showed that morning, that, above all else, he still enjoyed the game, and we must respect him for his decision to quit, in spite of it. Similarly, there was Peter Knowles, who retired at the height of his fame with Wolverhampton Wanderers to pursue his religious beliefs. Perhaps some people thought that he was just a silly, impressionable lad, but he made the decision and he had the courage to stick to it.

I remember one huge charity match in the Midlands for a little boy called Jamie Fellows, who was suffering from brain injuries sustained in tragic circumstances when he was just 16 months old. Both Knowles and Best were in the same team as me. It was the first game that Peter had played since his dramatic retirement, returning so as to help the little lad's cause and to have the chance to line up alongside George Best ... and me, of course!

When I arrived at Admiral's Park in Shifnal, the kit was neatly arranged on our pegs, hanging on coat hangers in a very professional manner. By coincidence, the Number 7 jersey, which was to be worn by George, was hanging next to the Number 2 shirt that I was wearing. So we began to get changed together. George, as usual, was quiet but friendly; but I noticed that the sparkle in his eyes was missing and that he was having to make an extra effort to laugh and joke with everybody.

It was really none of my business, but I quietly whispered to him as we pulled on our boots: 'Are you alright? You don't look too clever today.' He agreed that indeed he did not feel on top form, because he had received a traumatic telephone call in the middle of the night, to say that his son had been rushed to hospital. He had then driven through the night to Buckinghamshire, to sit up with Calum, holding his hand and, with the lad's mother Angie, had anxiously kept him company until it was time to drive up to Wolverhampton for this match, after which he would rush back to Buckinghamshire to be with his son again.

'You shouldn't have come,' I said. 'Everybody would have understood.'

'I didn't want to let the little fella's mother down, after all the work that Allan Phillips had put in to organize the game,' he replied, as we filed out onto the pitch.

The game was a great success: Best was brilliant, as always; I was the opposite – as always. Peter Knowles scored a great goal and a lot of money was raised to help Jamie's treatment. But there was not one single line in the national newspapers the following day to say that, despite agonizing personal problems, George Best had still made a super-human effort to turn up for this sick little boy.

He had the quickest shower possible at the end of the game, signed autographs for everybody and then dashed off back to the hospital. But, as he was leaving, he said to me as a parting shot: 'If you're not doing anything on Thursday evening, there's a big dinner being held in my honour, at a hotel in Stockport, 7.30, bow-tie job. You won't need a ticket – just turn up as my special guest.'

With that he was gone, off into the night.

As it happened, I could not go to the function but, the morning after it, I picked up the paper to read inch-high headlines screaming at me over my Cornflakes: BEST FAILS TO TURN UP FOR HIS OWN DINNER.

I felt very sad; the article, not surprisingly, casti-gated him for yet another non-appearance, but there was still no mention of his efforts for little Jamie Fellows, which was a shame. It seems that people only want to write about the more unsavoury and unfor-tunate incidents in George's life. But I know for a fact that there are many good things that he does that go totally unnoticed and certainly unreported.

There were 56,000 people in Wembley Stadium as Bobby Moore strolled in and began to get changed. He looked in good shape and obviously, by the relieved look on the face of Richard Keys, our gaffer had decided not to take any disciplinary action against the player for his late arrival.

The game itself was quite difficult for me in the

opening few minutes. I do not know whether it was the excitement, the heat, the lush turf, my age, or a combination of all four, but I was breathing through my mouth, my nose, my earholes and every other possible orifice, just to keep body and soul together. Frank Worthington, Malcolm Macdonald and Stan Bowles did not help matters much either, by constantly playing balls down my side of the field. However, I was comforted by the knowledge that Bobby was just alongside me and I quickly adjusted to the pace of things.

It is not so much how fast great players run, but it is the speed with which they move the ball around, even if they are a little past their sell-by date, that counts. And in this game they were knocking it around for fun, but it is not always the case. I remember a game at Crystal Palace: The North's Internationals v The South's Internationals ... I know! I know! I don't know what I was doing there either. Nevertheless, I was wearing the Number 3 shirt for The North. We had Alex Stepney in goal, Colin Bell, Mike Summerbee, Francis Lee, Bobby Charlton and David Sadler in our side, with the legendary John Charles playing at centre half. Jimmy Greaves captained the lads from The South, and his team contained Bob Wilson in goal, Frank McLintock, Terry Neill, Alan Mullery, Malcolm Macdonald and Jimmy Melia.

The only problem during this game was actually getting a kick of the ball. There were so many stars on parade that night that they all felt the need to do a little party piece every time they managed to gain possession of the ball, and they only released it when it was absolutely necessary. This did not unduly worry a bit player like me; I knew that the crowd most definitely had not paid money to see *me* perform, but I did not want the indignity of going through the entire 90 minutes without actually getting a kick and it was quite a relief when, after what had seemed an eternity,

65

Colin Bell slid me a completely unnecessary square ball with the words: 'Here Fred, have a kick for Christ's sake.'

What a nice boy he is!

To be honest, I cannot ever remember running about so much and achieving so little as I did in that game ... which really is saying something for me! And all I got for my pains were two extra-special bollockings from Bobby Charlton; one totally justified, one not.

The first came after we had conceded the first goal, which became inevitable after so much pressure. Bobby let me have it for not helping out John Charles enough and for failing to provide the great man with the extra cover that his age and standing in the game deserved. Believe me, if I could have done, I would have done. Nobody admired King John more than I did.

After about 20 minutes, for some reason known only to himself, comedian Stan Boardman, who was filming a TV series at that moment called *Some You Win*, decided that he would crawl along the touchline, microphone in hand, and conduct an on-the-spot interview with me, while the game was actually in progress.

'Fred?' I immediately recognized Stan's familiar Scouse voice and, even though it was early in the game, I thought that I was going to be substituted and, for once in my life, I would have been quite pleased to have been hooked off, because I could tell the way that things were going.

I looked round, fully expecting to see the Number 3 card held aloft, but instead I found myself staring into a TV camera and a boom microphone held by Stan.

'How's the game going?' was Stan's first penetrating question, as I quickly glanced over my shoulder to check that the ball was on the other side of the field. (Brian Moore has got nothing to fear, I thought ... but then again, neither had Kenny Sansom!) So off we

66

went. The red light was flashing, the camera was whirring and, while I hadn't a clue what it was all about, I went along with it.

'Well, not bad, Stan,' I gasped. 'I've enjoyed my one kick of the ball and hope to get another one before very long.'

I tried to jog away, but Stan persisted with the interview – it would have been more comfortable in a studio, I'm sure. But, just as I was once more looking over my shoulder, I heard two almighty roars, one from the crowd, the other from Bobby Charlton, who let me know in no uncertain terms that my second kick of the ball was on its way to me. I managed to retrieve it before it went out for a throw-in (that really would have been all that I needed), and then I knocked a decent ball upfield to little Keith Peacock and braced myself for a real roasting from Bobby.

I had to stand there and take it, of course, because he was right: the whole scenario was totally unprofessional, even though there really was nothing that I could have done to avoid it. Satisfied that he had made his feelings perfectly clear to me, Bobby galloped back upfield, still muttering to himself, leaving me to turn on Stan, who by this time was almost reeling about on the running track with glee. The camera was still rolling, but one look at Boardman's cheeky face was enough for me and I almost joined him, laughing on the track.

All in all it was not one of my better evenings, but at the end, as I sat in the dressing room, swigging a can of beer, it all seemed worthwhile as the great John Charles flopped down beside me, put a massive hand on my knee, squeezed it a little and said with a roaring laugh: 'You know Fred, you are without doubt the worst player that I've ever played with in my life.'

You know what? Coming from a player like John Charles, who has played with Sivori, Bonniperti, Roy

Paul and some of the greatest players the world has ever seen, that is one of the nicest things that anyone has ever said to me! And, whenever I see him, he always introduces me to his friends the same way.

In the game at Wembley, however, the ball was really being passed around. George Best, of course, was entitled to display a few tricks, but Currie was swinging balls all over the place and Bobby Gould was chasing about up front like a 20-year-old. It was a pleasure for me to play in such company. Unlike the game at Selhurst Park, I feel that I let myself down only once, when, I must confess, I became a little over-excited a few minutes before the end.

The score was 0-0, and it was obvious by their attitudes that, for most of the players, their pride had taken over, and nobody wanted to lose, even in a little game like this. Quite right too!

With only a couple of minutes left, Gordon Taylor, now chief executive of the PFA, hit a deep cross to the far post from the left wing. As soon as it left his foot, I knew that it was a quality ball. I also knew that Malcolm Macdonald was behind me on the far post, because I could hear him snorting and I could feel his breath on the back of my neck. He sounded how I felt, but that was no consolation to me, because I also knew that if that ball travelled its full distance, Supermac would be scrambling high on my back, while I would be struggling to slide even a copy of the *Daily Express* under my feet from a standing jump. I had visions of the net bulging to welcome yet another Supermac Wembley goal to go with the five record-breakers he scored against Cyprus in 1975. And I would be blamed for it, without a doubt.

My only hope was the keeper. If the ball eluded him, I was dead. I was painfully aware of that. Ray Cashley, the former Bristol City goalkeeper, thankfully sensed the danger and dashed off his line to punch the ball at full stretch, but it only caught the top of his knuckles and flew vertically high up into the air. It was still a dangerous situation, but in my usual selfish way, I was happy, briefly, because it had got me out of jail. Cashley's momentum had taken him out of the game, so we were now left with a six-yard box full of attackers and defenders, all looking upwards, waiting for the ball to drop down out of the sky in front of a gaping empty goal.

The ball had gone so high it had snow on it when it eventually came down and I was relieved it fell to Bobby Moore, who I was convinced would either knock it safely for a corner, or hook the ball wildly away over his shoulder, like any other mere mortal would have done.

I was getting quite panicky by now and, still with one eye on Macdonald on the far post, I screamed above the noise of the crowd: 'Just whap it, Bob,' as he watched the ball zooming down like one of the Red Arrows.

Facing his own goal, no more than a couple of yards out, he then proceeded to trap the ball and drag it back through his legs all in one movement, so that not only had he averted the immediate danger, but he also had the ball under perfect control, facing the right way. I was really impressed.

'Now whap it, Bob,' I screamed again, as he dummied past Chris Garland and played a neat one-two with me in my own penalty area.

'Bloody hell, Bob.' I was getting hoarse now, as I quickly gave it back to him before Malcolm clattered me.

He then played a majestic long ball upfield, reminiscent of the one that made Geoff Hurst and Kenneth Wolstenholme into living legends. He shook his head reproachfully at me and, with a little smile, said as we jogged upfield: 'Whap it? Whap it?!'

I really should have known better.

'Sorry Bob ... you and I have obviously not been playing the same game all these years!'

CHAPTER 9

The Centenary Cup Final

Wembley, to me, is the most magical stadium in the world. I have seen most of them: the San Siro, Benfica's Stadium of Light, Radcliffe Borough's Stainton Park, The Butchers' Arms, Droylsden! I have been on and played on plenty. But nothing can touch Wembley, and I sincerely hope that the game's legislators are never tempted to change the place or to build another super-modern national stadium in another part of the country, because our game would lose so much. Tart it up a bit by all means, spend some money on it, but do not do away with the place ... please!

Supporters always sing 'We're on our way to Wembley', they do not sing 'We're on our way to the Cup final'. Wembley is special, make no mistake about that. Most other countries who boast about their super-duper-domes are really quietly envious of our great stadium in the same way that they wish that they had their own Big Ben and their own Houses of Parliament, though not necessarily the people in there!

It takes many years to build a heritage and, thanks to policemen on white horses, Dick Pym, Frank Swift's fainting bout, Dixie Dean, Joe Mercer, Raich Carter, Peter Doherty, balls bursting, Jack Rowley, Wally Barnes, Stanley Matthews, Ronnie Allen's penalty, Ferenc Puskas, Nandor Hidegkuti, Jackie Milburn,

Bert Trautmann's broken neck, Peter McParland's brain-storm, Alan Taylor, Nat Lofthouse, Ronnie Boyce, Neil Young, Alan Sunderland, Norman Whiteside, Ian Rush and dozens more, Wembley Stadium definitely has a wonderful history and nothing can ever take that away.

Every visit I have ever made to a Cup final has, for me, been a truly memorable day, and I only wish that it was not quite so expensive these days for a father to take his son, because, if your team is playing, it is a day that you and your lad will remember for the rest of your life.

I have been to quite a few finals, the first being in 1958 when Bolton beat Manchester United and Nat Lofthouse scored the goals. I could not get a ticket when my own team, Manchester City, reached the final in 1955, 1956 and 1968. But in 1981 things were a little better for me, and I travelled down in style with my son Steven and my Dad to enjoy the Centenary Cup final, Manchester City v Tottenham Hotspur.

It was Steven's ninth birthday. He was soccer mad, a good little player for his age and a fanatical City supporter. His favourite player, Paul Power, was the captain of the team and other special favourites like Ray Ranson and Tommy Caton were also playing. Only two days earlier he had received a medal for his efforts in the Bury Junior Football League Under 11s team from Steve MacKenzie, who was also lining up against Spurs. As we settled into our seats, I hoped that MacKenzie would receive a winner's medal in return and make it a day that we would never forget. How right I was!

The match itself did not go according to plan. Tommy Hutchison scored a repeat of Bobby Johnstone's flying header in 1955, but then deflected a free kick past Joe Corrigan for a cruel own goal, and the match ended in a 1-1 draw.

Just about the time that we were in despair at Wembley, as the ball flew high past Big Joe into the net, 300 miles away in Manchester my wife Judith was cheerfully driving our daughter Suzanne back from a drama festival, when the car was hit head-on by another car driven by somebody who had obviously downed a few too many beers while watching the game on TV. I am told that the bang could be heard miles away, the impact was so great. Ambulancemen, policemen – everybody – rushed to the scene and, judging by the photograph in the following day's newspaper, it was difficult to imagine just how anybody could possibly have come out of it alive.

Fortunately, Suzanne had been flung clear of the wreckage, and any damage she suffered was not physical, but poor Judith bore the brunt of the whole disaster. After being cut free from the tangled mess that only a few seconds earlier had been a nice new car, she was lying in bits and pieces in the local hospital, fighting for her life, while the police set about trying to trace her husband.

As an extra treat for Steven and my Dad, I had decided to stay overnight in London. However, because most hotels were fully booked due to the Cup final, for once in my life I had not been able to let people know in advance where I would be staying and we were relieved to find a room at the Holiday Inn in Swiss Cottage. We had had a good day and were still blissfully unaware that it had not been so clever for the female half of my family. Steven and his grandad settled down to hamburger and chips in front of the TV set in their room to watch the game all over again on *Match of the Day*, hoping that the own goal had not really happened, while I drove a couple of miles up the road to Hampstead and enjoyed a lovely meal with journalist Peter Ball and his wife Sarah and Eamonn Dunphy, the little Republic of Ireland international inside forward. I had known Eamonn from my early days when I tried to pin him down, but he only used to laugh at me when we played against each other for City and United.

How the police tracked me down I do not know ... that Lord Lucan must be a clever guy, and Shergar must be even cleverer!

Nobody knew where we were. They must have rung Interpol, who would not have been very busy, because not many people want to send flowers in the middle of the night! But when I arrived back at the hotel, my Dad was waiting with the bad news: a team of surgeons in Manchester were contemplating amputating Judith's leg. So, in effect, some idiot gets legless and my wife was now heading the same way ... literally.

This was bad news indeed. I had only just bought her a new pair of wellies for her to use when digging the garden! I can laugh now, but it was certainly no laughing matter when I woke up Steven at 3.10 am to tell him that we had to rush back to Manchester because his Mum had been involved in a nasty accident. His little face at that moment will live with me for ever. One single tear dropped from his eye. Plop! onto his pyjamas. Just one tear, that's all, but it almost made me weep buckets as we set off up the M1. Dad looked grim, I looked grim, Steven looked bewildered:

Happy Birthday dear Steven,
Happy Birthday to you!

The journey up the motorway seemed to take a lifetime, but eventually I found myself outside Ward 5B at Withington Hospital, took a deep breath and walked in. The nurse, a lovely woman, told me to prepare myself for a shock. The specialist brought the X-ray, dropped it on the floor, trod on it with a big size ten shoe, dusted it off with his hand and held it up to the light for me to see: 'I'll have one ten by eight and two postcard size!'

73

I hope he's better with the knife, I thought, as he gruffly pointed at the picture of my wife's right leg, which at that moment did not look as though it would ever see a bikini again.

'As you can see, it's completely mashed,' he told me, waving his hand airily towards the negative. 'So we'll probably have to take it orf, but we're considering some very delicate traction work here, which may possibly save it. We're not quite sure.'

I was trying my best not to be the typical hysterical husband that I had seen so many times in situations like these in the movies. But this was for real, and I must admit that I was finding it a little difficult to keep myself under control while listening to such horrific news being explained to me in such a matter-of-fact way.

'This is not a potato we're talking about here, it's my wife's leg. Get the delicate traction work going, whatever that might be, and if that fails ... well ...' I left the rest of the sentence unsaid.

The decision was made – probably the quickest and best I will ever make in my life. I must confess that I did not like the specialist's attitude, his bedside manner would certainly not have won him a part in *Emergency Ward 10*. I will admit, though, that I did like his work, because the construction of the traction was nothing less than a masterpiece, like the Clifton suspension bridge. So I suppose I cannot complain. And thankfully Judith still has two legs. How they put it together again I will never know ... Humpty Dumpty obviously went to the wrong hospital!

Her other injuries eventually cleared up after many months in hospital, followed by painful, traumatic weeks trying to get herself upright again. And we all lived happily ever after. It had promised to be the Cup final we would remember, and that is certainly the way it turned out ... for all the wrong reasons.

74

CHAPTER 10

Oh dear! What can the matter be?

I was becoming quite a Wembley veteran. Only Stan Bowles has appeared there more times than me, he has not missed a greyhound meeting there for years! But I was certainly not becoming blasé about the fact, because something crazy always seems to happen to me whenever I go to the place.

The boss, Richard Keys, was proud to be one of the few managers not to get the sack that season. After all, his team had played just that one game in 12 months and had earned a creditable draw. And, let's be fair, any manager who goes a whole year and never loses a game is entitled to keep his job.

Richard decided that my debut had been a successful one and he kept me in the side for the next game, something that has not happened to me very often in the past, and I lined up with Bobby again, this time in Mansfield Town's colours, who were playing the holders Bristol City.

Again, it was another close encounter, another draw, with Richard himself scoring from the penalty spot to equalize David Johnson's good strike. It was another magic day, but again one where everything threatened to go hopelessly wrong for me. I won't even mention the horrendous traffic jams, my lunatic driving to make up

75

the lost time, policemen clearing Wembley Way for me while I drove down it the wrong way, on the pavement, simply to arrive in time for the kick-off. Whenever I think back to those couple of hours, I have to take two of my migraine tablets ... and when I think back to what came next, I have to take the whole bottle!

Judith had travelled down with me this time, to see her hero at Wembley. She thought it was a Cliff Richard concert! While she settled into her seat, I hurried to the dressing rooms. I was a bit harassed, the mad rush had not helped, but seeing all the great players in the dressing room calmed me down. Soon the bell sounded for us to go down and wait in the famous tunnel for the signal to take the field.

With the long journey from Manchester, arriving late, combined with a bit of nerves, I thought I had better make a quick dash to the toilet before taking the field, only to be told that the ones that we were using that day were halfway round the other side of the stadium. That was no good to me, and the more I thought about it, the more urgent became the need to go.

It is in moments of crisis such as these that Churchill, Montgomery and Blackley-born Wembley veterans separate themselves from the common herd. Knowing the geography of our great national stadium as I do, I thought I could quickly nip through the interview room, up a short flight of steps and into the referee's changing room where I could use his loo (he won't mind ... he'll have no choice, really ... at the worst it could only be a yellow card for not retreating ten yards).

Showing a neat change of pace, I whipped through the interview room glanced quickly at an idiot board, which already had 'I feel over the moon, Brian' written on it, in case any of the players ever forgot what to say next, then I bounded up the few steps and knocked on the ref's door.

No reply.

I pushed it open a little, peeped inside, but the room was empty. Three sets of clothes were hanging on their pegs, three hold-alls, with various odds and ends spilling out of them, three pairs of shoes tucked under the benches, but there was nobody in the room.

It is probably my suspicious nature, but under normal circumstances I would never enter a room like this, alone and unannounced, where other people's personal belongings were on display, because, no matter how innocent your intentions, if anybody else were to nip in there after you, rifle through the clothes and steal something, you really haven't got a leg to stand on if somebody were to say later: 'Oh, yes I saw him going in there.'

Try explaining that one away. So I always find it better not to put myself in that position in the first place, but I was desperate, so, after a moment's hesitation, I whizzed in and through to the little toilet in another room at the back: 'I'll be out in a couple of shakes!'

I thought I heard something click while I was standing there, but I did not take too much notice of it because I was concentrating on the job in hand. It could have been my knee. The old 'Francis Lee' had been giving me a bit of jip, but I realized it was not when I tried to turn the handle of the door to get out. Some silly, safety-conscious sod had locked me in. It was like something out of *Tales of the Unexpected*. I was due to play at Wembley in five minutes' time, I was fully kitted out – yellow shirt, socks, shorts and teeth to match – and here I was, locked in the referee's room.

I could faintly hear the noise of the crowd, over 60,000 of them blissfully unaware of my predicament, not that they would be bothered. But one of them, Judith, would be watching the two teams file out any second now, and one team would have 10 while the other had 11 ... and her husband would be the missing link.

I started to panic and looked round for a window.

77

There wasn't one. I looked round the little dressing room for something with which to force the lock – nothing. Referees and linesmen do not carry jemmies in their kit bags. I searched for something to smash the door down with – nothing. And then, to top it all, I heard the familiar sound of studs on concrete. I simply could not believe that this could be happening to me. That sound (together with the noise of the till in my shops!) is my favourite sound in the whole world, but on this occasion, it was a nightmare not a dream, because my studs should have been clinking down there in the tunnel with the rest of them, not trying to kick this door down.

'Alright! Alright! Keep your hair on,' said a voice from heaven. It seemed as though I had been in there for an eternity.

Click. It was the same sound as before, but this time I knew it was not my knee, as a fella wearing an orange fluorescent bib opened the door.

'What are you doing in there?' he demanded, as I pushed him out of the way and flew down the stairs.

My sweet, genteel riposte of 'Piss off' is not really what one would expect from an author, a wordsmith of repute, an after-dinner speaker who prides himself on his use of the English language, but it seemed to suit the occasion. Seconds later, I was galloping up the tunnel to join the end of my team as it strode proudly into the arena.

I cannot remember the first few minutes of the game, I was in a daze (so what's new?). I remember our keeper Alan Stevenson making a magnificent save from Bryan Hamilton and Emlyn Hughes playing well for them, but I must have done OK, because my man Bobby said to me at the end: 'Steady on Fred! Any more performances like that and you'll ruin your reputation ... people will begin to think that you're a good player.'

God forbid! I can't have that!

CHAPTER II

A geri-hat-trick

I celebrated my hat-trick of Wembley appearances the following season by captaining the 'Burnley' team against 'Wolves', and goals by Peter Noble enabled me to maintain my unbeaten record. It was especially pleasing for me to have Peter Noble and Nobby Stiles in my team that day, because it is a long time since there were two players in the same side as me with less hair than I have!

Leading a team out at Wembley Stadium in front of 86,000 wonderfully behaved fans just about did it for me. I now owe Richard Keys my house, my shops, both my legs, my back copies of *Football Monthly*, my autographed Real Madrid programme and a trip round the world on the QE2. He also wanted a scrap of paper that I have safely locked in a vault at the bank which says: 'Best Wishes, Doug Rougvie.' But I would not part with that!

Unfortunately, Burnley could not repeat the score in the big match. Steve Bull and Andy Mutch proved to be a little too powerful up-front for them, which was very disappointing all-round, because my son Steven was due to join the staff at Turf Moor when he left school in a few weeks' time, as a first-year YTS player, so naturally we hoped that he would be joining the winners of the Sherpa Van Trophy, but it was not to be.

Steven had been progressing quite nicely, although schoolboy football in the area was, at the time, quite frankly a joke. The teachers were taking industrial action by working to rule, so schools soccer, which had been so important to me and which I loved and looked forward to so much in my schooldays, was falling apart at the seams, and if it had not been for top-quality Sunday morning football, lads like Steven would probably have been lost to the game.

When schoolboy football in our area finally spluttered back to life again, the continuity had gone and I was horrified at what I had to witness. It was a total shambles, masquerading as trial games run by teachers, one of whom, a man in charge of Salford Boys, asked his friend to ring me up, requesting a list of football phrases that he could use to speak to the boys at half time.

'I can't tell him what to say about an imaginary game,' I protested. 'Every game is different.'

'He says it doesn't matter. Just give him a few sayings and he'll slip them in, the kids won't know what he's talking about anyway.'

I refused of course, and was choked to see that he was still one of the teachers in charge when Steven went along for his Salford Schoolboy trial.

So thank goodness for Sunday football! We were very pleased at the prospect of him joining a club like Burnley where, in the distant past, they had always placed the accent firmly on youth and the importance of finding and grooming their own young players.

Manchester United were one of the first of the recent crop of clubs to form a School of Excellence. Their first intake of boys, when the scheme was introduced, was for 12 youngsters aged 11, and Steven was one of that lucky dozen selected from the Salford, Bury, Oldham and Greater Manchester areas. Good, solid, professional coaching, and Steven loved it.

Training was held every Monday evening at The Cliff, and it was quite amusing to see this little lad in full Manchester City kit training with the others, who were all decked out in red and white. Steve never gave it a second thought, however, and coaches Eric Harrison, Jimmy Curran and the late Ray Woods used to pull his leg mercilessly about his allegiance to City. He became quite a little character there and really enjoyed his work under those three coaches, until Blackburn Rovers offered him the opportunity to sign schoolboy forms for them.

Manchester United were, as ever, very good about the whole thing. Ray Woods said they would like him to stay, but understood when we said that possibly there would be a little more scope for him at Blackburn and we have a lovely letter at home from the club saying what a pleasure it had been to coach the lad. Very nice. It probably took only a few minutes to write, but it is something else from the club that I will not forget.

Two years with Blackburn Rovers, one simply spent training and the other playing in the junior teams, would determine whether or not they thought that he would have the chance for a career in the game. But due to his slow physical development, they were two difficult years for the boy. Whenever he played, at some stage during every game he would show flashes of skill and vision that were not apparent in the other bigger, stronger, faster, more mature boys. But he was finding it hard to produce it consistently, because he was getting knocked about so much and was, as a result of this, struggling to keep pace with the game.

I just hoped that the club would plump for the skill and wait for him to grow up naturally, instead of signing the stronger, more powerful players in the hope that they could then teach them how to actually play and pass. I really did not know whether they would offer him a contract or not, but I was very anxious for them to do so because he loved the club, respected the coaches and manager, and was popular with the other players.

Any doubts I had, however, were laid to rest one cold January evening at Ewood Park when I bumped into one of the coaches and he told me how pleased he was with one or two of the youngsters, who would therefore be offered YTS places when they left school. Steven, he said, would be one of them. I was absolutely delighted, but it was such an important thing in my son's life that I thought I had better make doubly sure that I had heard him correctly, so I said slowly, in words of one and two syllables: 'So are you telling me that the club is definitely going to offer Steven a contract when he leaves school?'

To which he replied, and I quote: 'Unless we sign Maradona between now and the end of the season, we'll be offering Steve a YTS place.'

'Fine,' I said. 'But I won't say anything to him just yet, eh?'

'Yes, tell him by all means.'

Will I never learn?

After all the crap that I have had to swallow throughout my career, you would think that I would have known better, wouldn't you? So I did what any other dad would do to a soccer-mad kid. I drove home, very excited at the prospect of telling him that the first part of his dream had come true, and that he now had one foot (in his case, the left one) on the very bottom rung of the ladder. I woke him up, actually woke him up instead of leaving it until the following morning, and told him the good news.

He was so thrilled that he could not get back to sleep again – but what the hell!

Well, Blackburn Rovers did not sign Maradona ... they did not sign Steven Eyre either, which is their prerogative. I only wish that they had not told me that they were going to do so, and I wish, even more, that I had kept my big mouth shut, because that made it even harder for the boy to come to terms with his disappointment.

Most youngsters suffer some form of disappointment during their formative playing years. It is something that is not very pleasant to see, but it does help to build their character. Many sustain an injury and miss a big chunk of their all-important first season, leaving themselves with too much leeway to make up. The most common single complaint nowadays for sports-minded kids is Osgood Schlatters' Disease – severe inflammation around the knee joints. (It was called growing pains when I was young!) It is painful nevertheless, and often any form of sporting activity is forbidden by the doctor for anything up to a year, until it eventually clears itself up.

It is amazing how many youngsters suffer with this problem, not to be confused with Osgood Over-the-top Disease, which was also diagnosed by a severe pain around the knee joint after being on the receiving end of a slightly late tackle, usually in the Stamford Bridge area of London or around The Dell at Southampton, when Peter was starring for Chelsea and the Saints respectively.

One of the unluckiest kids missed his way however, not through injury, loss of form, or lack of ability. He was a young centre half who played with Steve as an associate schoolboy for two seasons, giving his all, just like the rest of them, to try to impress the club sufficiently enough for them to offer him a YTS place. When decision-time came, he was one of the unfortunate ones who was not offered a contract. I mentioned in passing to one of the coaches in charge that he must have only just missed the boat, because I thought that he had progressed quite well.

He agreed with me that he was in fact a borderline

case and added that he thought that he might be a little bit small to become a top-class centre half. He said that they did, at one point, consider signing him anyway, in the hope that he would grow those extra few inches. He finally received the thumbs down from this coach, however, because he said that he always looked closely at the fathers of all of his boys, because it gave him some idea what size their offspring were likely to be when they eventually finished growing, and this lad's father was not a giant by any stretch of the imagination. So, in effect, the boy was denied his chance because of his father's height.

It is a good job that Ronnie Corbett had two daughters, because a son of his would have no chance in the game according to him! I could not say, of course, whether his theory would prove to be right or wrong, but I felt a bit sorry for the boy and his father, with whom I had spent many wet hours shivering on various touchlines most Saturday mornings for the previous two years. So I decided to ring him up and say how sad I was that his youngster had just missed out. When I looked up his name in the telephone directory, I could not find it, but eventually managed to obtain it from a mutual friend and gave him a ring.

'Hello,' I said. 'It's easier getting hold of the Pope. I couldn't find you in the telephone directory?'

He laughed. 'That's probably because you don't know my name.'

I confessed that I did not understand.

'We have different surnames, my son and I. I am his stepfather, you see, and he wanted to retain his own name.'

I was too stunned to speak. Certainly it was not for me to tell him the reason why his stepson was not being given the opportunity of becoming a professional footballer. His natural father might have had the physique of Terry Butcher, so that put paid to the coach's clever theory. Unfortunately, this theory had also put paid to the lad's chances of a career in the game. I genuinely hope that he gets another chance in the future when he is six foot two and weighs 13 stone!

Fortunately for Steven, Burnley, in the shape of Welsh international Leighton James, threw him a lifeline and he was due to report to Turf Moor a few weeks after the big day at Wembley. So naturally, as I disappeared down the tunnel for the last time, I hoped that Burnley would win.

The two teams were lined up ready to take the field. What a marvellous day for them! I had merely played in an insignificant curtain-raiser and I felt as though I had just won the World Cup, so to be going on there to play in a big game really must be a fabulous feeling.

I did not know many of the Wolves players personally. Captain Aly Robertson was at the head of the line, a wily old campaigner. I shook hands with goalkeeper Mark Kendall, a super lad that I knew from his days at Newport, and that was it as far as the Wolves team was concerned. But I knew, liked and respected most of the Burnley players. Skipper Ray Deakin, Steve Gardner, Steve Taylor, George Oghani and Peter Daniel were all players I had known for a very long time, and I genuinely wanted them to do well as I wished them good luck and watched them walk up the tunnel into the sunshine and the deafening roar from the crowd.

I hung about for a second and had a last look round, for I knew that, at my age, it would be my last time there. I admit that it was not what I had planned when I dreamed of playing there as a kid, but I have been more than happy to settle for it.

I did actually play at Wembley. I did actually lead a team out there and I also picked up an FA Cup Winners' medal there in the Royal Box – but, unfortunately, it wasn't my own!

CHAPTER 12

Merseyside is wonderful

This is the only way to watch a Cup final, I thought, as I settled into my plush seat in the Royal Box, with Sir John Moores seated next to me on my right-hand side wearing a blue and white Everton scarf around his neck and Sir Matt Busby on my left. It was a far cry indeed from what I had been used to as a kid – a 12-inch black and white TV set, a glass of shandy and a bag of chocolate caramels, when my eyes would never leave the screen for a second. That was how Cup final day used to be for me – and I loved it, hoping that one day it would be my turn.

Today, however, things were a little different, thanks to Graham Kelly, secretary of the Football League – or should I say Mrs Kelly? It was her indisposition that had led to Graham inviting me to the game as his personal guest. Now being substitute at Wembley would normally be something of a coup for me, but to be sub for a lady, even a nice one like Mrs Kelly, was a new departure, even for an experienced Number 12 like me, who had made the position fashionable long before David Fairclough came along to make a career out of it.

I really do not know why Mr Kelly invited me, with the whole of the football world at his feet, but I accepted the offer as graciously as it was offered and arrived in my best clobber ready for anything.

The pre-match luncheon, attended by football's top brass, was splendid, though not the best meal I have ever had at a football match by any means – Len Hilton's pies at Rochdale on a freezing December night take a lot of beating. But, nevertheless, I enjoyed it, even if the smoked salmon was a little salty!

It was Everton v Manchester United, and it promised to be an entertaining game, with two good sides packed out with international players. I considered myself to be an authority on both teams, having seen them play many times that season and, as such, I was invited to travel to Liverpool on the Thursday prior to the big game to discuss the final, and football in general, on Radio Merseyside's *Billy Butler Show*.

Billy Butler, a staunch Evertonian, had, by this time developed a cult following in the Merseyside area with his early morning show, a mixture of chat and easy-on-the-ear music, punctuated by Billy's humour and general knowledge of most topics.

The job of keeping the show under control and steering it in the right direction fell to producer Wally Scott, who succeeded in making a difficult job seem so easy that he too was fast becoming a personality in his own right and was contributing more and more to the show while on air. He also managed to attend to the behind-the-scenes problems that crop up by the minute during a live radio show – especially this one! Indeed, so popular was Billy and Wally's phone-in programme, *Hold Your Plums*, that their telephone conversations with Liverpudlian housewives have become legendary.

The two lads seem to have developed the knack of picking out the Les Dawson/Roy Barraclough-type gossiping housewife to go on air and then they tie her in knots with their repartee, as well as producing fabulous radio entertainment into the bargain. Only the previous week a lady contestant had phoned in to the studio to take part in Billy's record quiz and was going along quite nicely until she was asked: 'Who made the record "The Lion Sleeps Tonight"?'

She hesitated and said she knew it but could not quite think of the answer and, in desperation, asked Billy for a little clue. As the band was called Tight Fit, he replied: 'OK, love. I'll give you a clue: think of your husband's underpants.'

The women shrieked with delight: 'I've got it, Billy ... The Dooleys!'

A scriptwriter would pay fortunes for stuff like that and Billy brings it out of ordinary people every single day. I felt quite at ease as I settled in opposite the aforementioned Mr Butler in his tiny studio in Paradise Street. For some reason, I am always very well received in Liverpool, I have spoken at many functions in the city, appeared frequently on both the local radio stations and always the reaction is great and everyone is very friendly towards me, which is not always the case when a Woollyback crosses the boundaries of the city. Maybe they are all simply grateful that I never played for either of their great teams.

Billy was smiling as usual, Wally was giggling as usual and I knew, when the studio clock struck 11.30, that it had been a great show. Billy had made me sound good, by asking me all the questions that he realized would bring the best out of me and, with Wally chipping in incessantly and laughing in all the right places, I knew that I had done well. So much so, that during the news break, Wally asked me to stay on a little longer and judge the Everton Fancy Dress Parade that Radio Merseyside was hosting live at that very moment in the reception area. 'Do you think that you could handle something like that?' he said.

Fancy asking me a question like that.

'Course I can!' I replied, the adrenalin still running

high after my mini-success a few minutes earlier. I visualized myself as a sort of Wogan, Parkinson and Aspel all rolled into one ... What a thought!

While they played the first record after the news break, I trailed the microphone through to the reception area and was quite taken aback by the sight. The place was absolutely packed with people in a variety of fancy costumes, each appertaining to Everton Football Club. There was a lady in a blue and white crinoline dress with a basket of toffees, to denote the club's nickname, The Toffeemen; there was another lady with dozens and dozens of fake Cup final tickets pinned all over her from head to foot; there was a man painted silver, with massive false ears and a teapot lid on his head (I thought he was supposed to be Prince Charles ... but he was in fact a replica of the FA Cup); there was a Welshman with a stick stuck up his bum who was there as Taffy Apple!

No! No! That's not true! I just got a bit carried away there! But you name it, and I swear that they were all crammed into this room. I was rather fortunate with the two people that I selected to interview, as I contrived to pick two that could actually speak! I had a bit of fun with them and then picked the winner, a lady, and presented her with her prize, two precious tickets for Saturday's FA Cup final at Wembley.

What a wonderful morning's work; everything had been broadcast live, I had lived off my wits (not a lot to go off there!) and provided a really good morning's entertainment for the listeners. So I was feeling full of my little self as I began to wrap up the episode and was in full flow, a little more like Richard Dimbleby by now ... at least around the waist!

'Well, it's a magnificent sight here at Radio Merseyside. It's a sea of blue and white, some magnificent costumes on show here, obviously a tremendous amount of work has gone into the making of all of these costumes, but I'm sure that if you were down here and could see with your own eyes, you would agree with me that I have picked a worthy winner, and with that ...', and I was just about to say 'I'll hand you back to Billy Butler' when this little old lady tugged at my sleeve and, with a Scouse accent as thick as a navvy's butty, said quite aggressively for such a frail-looking little thing: 'Eh? I thought dat yer would interview me, 'cos my son's Ed Stewart.'

I stopped in full flow. If I had not been feeling so cocky, I would have ignored her, handed back to Billy and would have been halfway back up the East Lancs Road by then. But no! I took up the challenge and said: 'Well, before we go back to Billy, let's have a quick word with Ed Stewart's mum.'

Now, like Michael Caine, I store up lots of useless little bits of information that nobody else could really care less about – there is only one Monopolies' Commission, for example, not a lot of people know that! – and, as soon as she mentioned Ed Stewart, a little bell rang in my computer and I thought that I would enlighten the listeners with one or two words of wisdom regarding Stewpot, most children's favourite disc jockey of the day on Radio One.

'I'm sure that all the listeners know that Stewpot is a great Everton fan, in fact, if my memory serves me correctly, he did lead the community singing one year before the FA Cup final at Wembley. Will he be doing the same again this year, or is he going to the game just as a fan, like everybody else?'

I bent down a little so that she could answer into the microphone: 'Wot yer talkin' about?'

I knew, at that precise moment, that I was in deep trouble. I did not know what it was going to be, but I could sense that I was in it right up to my neck. Still, there was nothing that I could do, it was live radio, maybe a million listeners, I just had to take a deep

How many can you pick out? Malcolm Macdonald, Frank Worthington, Brendan Batson, Gordon Taylor, Ralph Coates, David Webb, Stan Bowles, Mickey Burns, Chris Garland, Peter Bonetti, Bobby Gould, Gerry Gow, Bobby Moore, Terry Mancini, George Best, Fred Eyre, Graham Kelly, Ray Cashley, Tony Currie, Bill McMurdo; and from TV-am: Richard Keys, Mike Morris, Jim Ferguson and Gary Imlach.

Mickey Burns and Stan Bowles trying the old one-two against me at Wembley. George Best is lurking upfield, waiting for me to win the ball. He had a bloody long wait!

I hope that this was the serious part of my speech! Either that or Bobby Charlton and Graham Kelly have been drinking vodka and Bostik. *(Bob Thomas)*

With compère Neil Midgley. The soda syphon soon washed the smile off my face. *(Denise Plum News-Sport)*

Bobby Mitchell – a wizard and a gentleman for Newcastle United, before my tackle almost maimed him for life. *(A. Wilkes & Son)*

Sammy Nelson getting 'behind' the Coventry City defence.

Paul Stewart in his Manchester City days. I am the president of his fan club.
(Bob Thomas)

It must be something in the
jeans! Father and son – a young
hopeful and a never was.

Mickey Quinn reminding
everyone how many thousands
of pounds Wigan Athletic gave to
Stockport County to take him off
their hands.

Richard Keys – I hope he never cashes in the debts that I owe him.

'I'll be Frank with you Fred, if only we could have signed you for Arsenal, who knows what we might have achieved.' An intimate discussion with Mr McLintock.

Book-signing sessions. Right: Sir Stanley Matthews still draws them in. Below: I cannot compete with Stan, but at this point I am at least drawing 2-2 with Mike McCartney.

Piccadilly Radio's Breakfast Show. Never work with children, animals and the wonderful Dave Ward. *(Studio Life)*

Lunch with Tommy Gore...who needs a friend like me?

breath and plough on: 'I'm talking about your son,' I replied, inwardly cringing, 'because you've just told us that your son is Ed Stewart.'

'He is,' she snapped, almost biting my head off in the process, 'at Goodison Park every Saturday; he's in charge of all the stewards!'

I felt my legs go, my top lip stuck to my teeth. If you live by the sword, you have got to be prepared to die by it, and this old dear had just knocked every ounce of cockiness out of me in one fell swoop. It ruined a good day's work and I could not wait to skulk off back to Manchester, where I would have a better chance of understanding just what people were actually saying to me! What is it about the *Billy Butler Show*?

CHAPTER 13

What a load of rubbish!

The FA Cup final of 1985 was a fairly uneventful affair, except for two major incidents: Norman Whiteside's tremendous individual goal to win the game and the controversial decision by referee Peter Willis to propel Manchester United's Kevin Moran into the record books by making him the first player ever to be sent off in an FA Cup final at Wembley.

Whiteside's effort was superb – a goal fit to win any Cup final and I probably had a better view of the shot than anybody else in the whole of the stadium – certainly better than Everton keeper Neville Southall! From my seat in the Royal Box, I was directly behind Norman, as he faked to go down the right touchline, checked inside and curled a left-foot shot round a defender and aimed for Southall's cap and gloves, tucked just inside the far post. It was a fantastic effort, and one which only a naturally left-footed player like the Irish international would even have been able to contemplate, let alone execute, to such perfection.

By this time, of course, United were down to ten men. Everton's Peter Reid had been unceremoniously upended in midfield by Moran as he took route one to goal and, while there was no real danger, because Reid still had about 20 yards to run before he would have got within striking range, and Percy Sugden probably could have caught Peter over that distance, referee Willis had no hesitation in dismissing the Reds' central defender.

On this occasion, the ten men battled just that bit harder than Everton, with their full quota. Frank Stapleton dropped back into the heart of United's defence, drew upon his vast experience of the big occasion and, thanks to Whiteside's goal, helped steer Manchester United to an unexpected victory against all the odds.

I was within touching distance of the FA Cup as it was handed over to Bryan Robson – the nearest I have ever been to my favourite piece of silverware – and could see first-hand the delight on the faces of the players as they were each handed their treasured winners' medals. By the time Kevin Moran filed up to receive his, all eyes, mine included, were upon Robbo as he raised the Cup triumphantly above his head for the benefit of the red army of fans, who, as usual, had travelled down from Manchester. So I did not see or hear Kevin Moran being told the bad news that any player sent off in an FA Cup final did not receive his medal.

It was obviously an archaic ruling that had never previously had cause to be brought into operation, but no doubt as soon as Kevin received his marching orders, some little bureaucrat from the FA was whooping with glee at the prospect of enforcing it for the first time in over a hundred years. However, I was blissfully unaware that Kevin Moran did not have his winners' medal in his sweaty palm, as I watched the overjoyed United players cavorting around the arena on the customary lap of honour.

By this time I was the only person left in the Royal Box. The true football inhabitants had slowly drifted away discussing the merits of the game and all its finer points, while the rest, those people who only attend one game a season, had made a bolt for the hospitality suite before the sausage rolls could cool down and had downed a few glasses of wine before the last disappointed Everton player had even received his losers' medal. I was happy where I was. I could drink wine and eat sausage rolls anywhere in the world, but I knew that I would never again sit in the Royal Box at Wembley, so I was in no hurry to leave.

The stadium was still and empty. It was quite eerie really, considering that only minutes earlier the place had been throbbing with 100,000 screaming football fans and now there was only me and the members of the groundstaff, who were sweeping the littered terraces. It was amazing how everybody had left the scene so quickly. I had never seen a crowd disperse so rapidly since George Poyser was manager of Manchester City!

I had a last look around. I had not been disappointed, the atmosphere in there was as regal as I thought it would be. The velvet ledge, where the Cup stands before the winning captain gets his hands on it, looked as imposing as ever, even though I think that the patch where Bobby Moore wiped his hands before receiving the World Cup in 1966 should have been preserved for posterity.

The Royal toilet came as a bit of a surprise. I had never really thought of that, but I suppose it stands to reason really; we cannot all have a Royal flush! In fact, the only major disappointment to me was that, ten minutes before the end of the game, a flunky brought up the medals from the bowels of the stadium in a Heinz baked beans carton and plonked the box right next to the FA Cup for the presentation. Now I had not, up until that point, given the small matter of how the medals actually reached the Royal Box much thought. Possibly, I expected them to be nicely set out on a velvet cushion, but certainly I did not expect, with all due respect to Heinz, to see FA secretary Ted Croker dipping his hand into one of their cartons amid all the pomp and circumstance.

Still, I am sure that the players did not mind, so long as they each received one, and I gave the matter little thought as a member of the groundstaff began sweeping around my ankles. Obviously there was not much litter in the Royal Box – the type of person who sits in there takes their litter home with them. There was, of course, the odd empty caviar tin and the stubs of a few Havana cigars left behind. These, along with the baked beans carton, were all swept together in a neat pile of rubbish, as the steward swung his legs back over the Royal Box and onto the terracing to continue his thankless sweep around the stadium.

I decided to make a move but, as I made my way to the exit, I paused for only a second to slip back to my childhood and aim a playful kick at the carton to see if I could curl it the way that Norman had done only an hour earlier. The carton flew in one direction, a little box whizzed out in the other. I bent down to investigate further, opened the little box and there, gleaming at me, was a beautiful gold medal, the size of a two-bob piece, with the word 'WINNER' inscribed upon it. That word alone indicated that it could not possibly be mine! But what was it all about? Who could it possibly belong to?

While one of the Everton lads might have been too disappointed to go up for his medal, this was a winners' medal and surely all the members of the winning team had collected theirs? I simply could not work it out, but I slipped it quickly into my pocket before it was swept away forever, and then set about deciding what to do next.

When I reached the banqueting room, the first person I saw was Bobby Charlton and quietly I told him that I had an FA Cup winners' medal in my pocket, but there were so many people around him, patting him on the back, driving him mad as usual that I do not think he really took on board what I was telling him, because he simply smiled that famous smile and said 'Good lad', and I was left with the thing still burning a hole in my pocket. Eventually, I found my man Graham Kelly and told him the whole story. He found the entire sequence of events quite unbelievable, but had to admit defeat when I surreptitiously slipped the medal into his hand.

As the world now knows, Kevin Moran was privately presented with his medal the following week after the FA kindly decreed that he could have it. Just what they would have presented him with if I had not lingered in the Royal Box after the game, I do not know. But I presume that there were one or two red faces at Lancaster Gate when Graham handed the medal to one of the officials and explained what had happened.

I do not know if the procedure has changed since 1985 – I still think a velvet cushion or a silver tray is the correct thing for the job – but knowing which way the game is going these days, the medals are probably still brought up in a brown cardboard box, but nowadays companies will be charged for having their names printed on it. A good idea ... but Heinz beans got wind of it first!

CHAPTER 14

On the Eyre waves

As so often happens with me, I slipped into the world of radio by accident. Following my appearances on a variety of local and BBC radio shows throughout the country as a studio guest, discussing either my books or football in general, I was asked to cover matches as an analyst every Saturday afternoon for Piccadilly Radio, Greater Manchester's own local radio station.

I thought that Picc' was, at the time, a throbbing, vibrant station, full of bright new ideas, a place bursting at the seams with inventive, talented people under the guidance of programme controller Tony Ingham, a man who possessed the knack of unearthing unlikely characters, giving them a break and guiding them to big things. So I was very pleased to place myself in his capable hands.

I had, over the years, listened to many people discussing football through the media. Some I thought were good, most were not so good and one or two were absolutely appalling. So, while I had received no formal training as such, it was agreed that I did possess a suitable face for radio and that I instinctively knew what was required. I decided to give the listener exactly what I thought he or she – mostly he in my case – wanted to hear: interesting, factual, informative material regarding the job in hand, football, explained in terrace language (minus the expletives!) that all could understand and identify with.

I felt that I had a head start, of course, with my profound knowledge of the game! This, plus my ability to store up details and obscure facts relating to most clubs and players both past and present, would, I thought, stand me in good stead. It was not until I began the job, however, and mingled with my colleagues, that I realized that the vast majority of them had little interest in the game and, therefore, even less knowledge. Many of the men crammed into the rabbit hutches that masquerade as press boxes up and down the country seemed to me to be journalists who had been assigned to a football match, rather than football writers specializing in the game and who at least pride themselves in having some knowledge of the job.

As far as they were concerned, it could have been births, marriages and deaths ... hatch 'em, match 'em and dispatch 'em. It did not matter what it was, they would simply go along and report on what they saw. The fact that they did not appear to know the names of any of the 22 players on view and struggled to come to terms with the soccer scene in general seemed totally irrelevant.

'There's always the programme,' they used to say, when I commented on their lack of knowledge. And it never ceased to amaze me when I sat and watched match reporters reading from the pen pictures in the match magazine and getting fact after fact totally wrong.

One chap at Burnden Park, Bolton, asked me before he went on air if Leeds United, the visitors, had any famous players in the team that day. As far as I was concerned, they were all famous, but, as we were in Lancashire, I picked out one or two for him with Manchester connections. I could have told him Arthur

Askey was playing centre half. He obviously hadn't got a clue.

However, happy to oblige, I said: 'Well, there's Andy Ritchie – he used to play for Manchester United; and Kevin Hird, they signed him from Blackburn Rovers.' I then scanned the teamsheet, looking for a couple of names that I thought that he could possibly pronounce correctly, like Smith or Brown.

Also playing that day was Paul Hart, who I had known since he was a little boy, as he is the son of my former coach at Manchester City, Johnny Hart. Paul, a big, strapping centre half, had begun his career at Stockport County, moved on to Blackpool, and had recently joined Leeds for a £350,000 fee and I instinctively told my man '... and of course there's Johnny Hart's lad. He's just come to Leeds for 350 grand.'

'Thanks a lot, Fred,' he said, and scurried away to the press box to broadcast his opening piece.

As the players came out onto the field, I settled into my seat in the row behind him and was quite astounded by the confident manner in which he addressed his listeners, considering that he knew absolutely nothing about his subject. He extolled the virtues of this great Leeds club, reading directly from the match programme. He proceeded to tell his spellbound listeners at home that 'this Yorkshire side has a sprinkling of Lancashire steel in it these days, with the inclusion of striker Andy Ritchie, well-remembered in these parts for his goal-scoring feats for Manchester United. He's joined by Kevin Hird, the former Blackburn Rovers player. But the star of the team at the moment must surely be centre half Johnny Hartslad. Hartslad was signed recently from Blackpool for £350,000 and he has really strengthened the team.'

As soon as he had finished his bit, I tapped him on the shoulder and he looked round at me with a confident, arrogant, self-satisfied, smug, big-time-Charlie look on his face. I paused for a moment, sighed to myself and said: 'It doesn't matter.' I listened to this sort of thing week after week and could not believe how they could possibly continue to get away with it.

Richard Keys had always been head of sport at Piccadilly during my time there. In my opinion, he was the ideal man for the job: hard-working, articulate, smart, knowledgeable and he was always very fair and honest towards me. It was obvious that he was destined for bigger things, and so it turned out. He moved into the world of television and, as far as I am concerned, he was a sad loss to the station and to me. He also spoiled me, because he knew his job and I foolishly believed that everybody else in his position was the same. Wrong again!

After his departure, there was a period when I worked for whichever radio station rang me first. Consequently, the instructions that I was receiving were coming from all directions, and I am definitely not at my best taking orders from people who seem to know nothing about the subject that they are in charge of. Thus it was one particular morning when I sat opposite a man who was intent on teaching me a bit more about football – after all, he had been watching the game for three weeks now!

He rolled his pencil between his fingers (you know the situation) and, pausing for maximum effect, he eventually said: 'Fred, I want you to cover this Saturday's game at Shrewsbury Town.'

'OK,' I replied. This was not really startling news, it hardly warranted a call to the office, but he was new in the job and Saturday's game was only an excuse to talk to me. Although he knew, within himself, that he did not possess any of the natural attributes for the job, he realized that he could fool most of the people most of the time. However, he understood that he would struggle to impress me, so he thought that he would try to astound me with his knowledge.

'Soooo,' he continued, drawing out the word as all the best executives do on TV. 'I've rung through to Meadow Lane and arranged for a ticket to be left for you at the players' entrance. Will that be alright?' I even detected a slightly patronizing tone creeping in, as he grew in self-confidence.

I never batted an eyelid.

At that moment I decided that my relationship with him and his radio station would definitely be short-lived and I also realized the reason why so many mistakes go out over the air: the men who think that they are in charge do not know any better.

Now a nice person would simply have corrected his mistake quietly. Obviously, it would appear that I am not the nice person that my Mother thinks I am, especially when I am dealing with somebody like this, trying to fanny his way through life. I simply had no sympathy, and even less respect, for him.

'Fine,' I replied, 'but I'd better leave extra-early on Saturday if I've got to drive to Notts County to pick up the ticket from Meadow Lane, and then get across to Shrewsbury Town in time for the game at Gay Meadow.'

He at least had the good grace to blush a little, but he still did not have enough sense to avoid doing the very same thing again a few weeks later. This time he was leaning on the photocopying machine in the corridor as I walked by. 'Fred,' he shouted after me.

I took a deep breath and turned around, he really did get on my nerves. 'Port Vale on Saturday. How long will it take you to get to South Wales?'

I wonder what school he went to?

'I don't think you know your Port Talbot from your Ebbw Vale,' I replied. 'Port Vale is actually in the Potteries.'

'I thought that was Stoke City,' he said.

101

From that day on, nothing really surprised me. Only a week later I heard one scribe in the press box, again reading a pen picture from the programme, pick out one particular player as the danger man for his team that day, which was unfortunate because, since the programme had been printed, the player in question had been transferred to another club. And he, of course, did not know this.

I really tuned in, however, with extra-special interest one day in my car, when I learned that the legendary Bert Trautmann, Manchester City's most famous player of all time, had made a surprise visit to the club, totally unannounced, from his home in West Germany. Trautmann, just about the best goalkeeper I have ever seen, was, as most people know, a former German paratrooper who, following his capture during the war, remained in this country and captured our hearts with his great goalkeeping displays and his warm personality. He had broken his neck diving at the feet of Birmingham City's Peter Murphy during the 1956 FA Cup final and, in recent years, he had travelled the world working for the German Football Federation, coaching soccer and generally being a fine ambassador for his country.

Now, briefly, he was back where he had spent his entire playing career, at Maine Road, where an intrepid reporter had spotted him and nabbed him for an impromptu interview, which ended with a never-to-be-forgotten question. It was not: 'Now that East Germany has joined with West Germany, how are we ever going to get a place by the pool?' It was even more embarrassing than that.

'Bert, you are generally regarded as the finest goalkeeper of all time, but you never played for England, why was that?'

Honestly! I nearly crashed my car.

I hoped that Bert would say: 'Because I'm German,

you stupid, incompetent *dumbkopf*.' But he is too much of a gentleman for that, of course, and he waffled on and stammered and stuttered his way through an answer, simply to avoid embarrassing the fool.

Really, if you are a sports reporter, there is no excuse for that sort of thing – or for discussing the merits of Scottish football if you know nothing about the game north of the border either. On this occasion, two 'experts' were discussing the merits of Scottish football, the wealth of Glasgow Rangers, and the extravagant spending of their manager Graeme Souness, when one of them, in an effort to enlighten his apparently ignorant listeners, said: 'Yes, but don't forget that Rangers attract crowds of over 40,000 every other week to Ibrox, so they can afford to spend all of that money, whereas smaller clubs like ...'

Wait for it! Now he could have said Cowdenbeath, Stenhousemuir, Albion Rovers, East Fife, Stranraer or any number of smaller Scottish clubs, but he went for Third Lanark, as confident and as knowledgeable as you like! '... they only get crowds of one and two thousand people watching them every week, so it's no wonder that they don't have any money to spend on transfer fees.'

Third Lanark, that great little club that sent Alex Harley, Matt Gray and Dave Hilley down to English football, had sadly gone out of existence approximately 14 years previously. There's a housing estate on the ground now I believe, so it is no wonder that they have no money to buy any players. I just wonder where the 2,000 people are going who trample through that estate every other Saturday.

Actually, it is an insult to the intelligence of the listener if they think that this sort of thing goes unnoticed. And, while it is apparently fair game to criticize the big boys like John Motson, Brian Moore, Martin Tyler and Alan Parry, let's be honest, you never hear them making gaffes like that, because, love them or hate them, they know their stuff. They do their homework and generally give the listener or the viewer correct and interesting information.

I decided from the word go that I would try to have as much fun with the job as possible. I would give serious, considered opinions, of course, but inject a bit of humour whenever possible, especially at the expense of the players.

I love footballers, their humour and their resilience. You have to have lived the life of a footballer to fully understand what I mean. Indeed, it is probably because I know most of them so well that I found it easy to poke a little bit of fun in their direction, whenever the opportunity presented itself, perfectly safe in the knowledge that they know me well enough to realize that it is only a little bit of harmless banter.

There were odd times, of course, when my comments landed me in a little bit of tepid water. But that never bothered me much. One such occasion came during a game at Anfield. Liverpool were in front, but Spurs were not taking things lying down and had attacked from the very first whistle and, indeed, in an attempt to force the game their way, they made an attacking substitution late in the match by taking off young Scottish winger Alistair Dick and replacing him with Garth Crooks. I knew that it would get me in trouble, but it was too good an opportunity to miss, so I told the listeners: 'Spurs are maintaining their attacking policy, right to the bitter end, with Garth Crooks replacing Alistair Dick and, judging by his performances while on loan to Manchester United recently, any United fans listening might well say that they have taken off one Dick and replaced him with another.'

It wasn't true of course, Garth is a terrific footballer. But never let the truth get in the way of a good line, that's my motto. And it is true to say, with my hand on my heart, that if I did not know Garth Crooks personally and know him to be a super, articulate, kind, thoughtful lad, I would not have said it. I knew that he would only have a chuckle if anybody related it to him. However, the expected memo from the boss was waiting on my desk for me when I arrived on Monday morning.

Ray Ranson, another good pal of mine, announced in the press that he wanted a transfer 'because he was fed up at being treated like a piece of the furniture'. It was my job to comment on this startling piece of soccer news and I could only observe that I did not feel that this was the case, because I had never seen a piece of furniture that only had one leg!

Ray didn't mind. 'At least I'm not a piece of antique furniture like you,' he said the next time I saw him. 'The last time that you went to a transfer tribunal, Arthur Negus set the transfer fee!'

Of course, the Bolton Wanderers players had to suffer a bit, because I covered all of their games and, indeed, travelled on the team bus. Big Gerry McElhinney was my usual target – the things that man couldn't do with a ball! But what a great lad he is, and what a competitor to have in your side ... or next to you in the trenches. He will admit himself that while he and Alan Hansen both play in the same position, that is just about the only similarity – except, of course, for their international caps proudly displayed at home. Which just goes to prove that there is room in the game for all kinds of players.

On one occasion at Stamford Bridge, right back Neil Berry was having a particularly difficult time against Chelsea's flying winger Peter Rhoades-Brown, to such an extent that, as the fourth goal went in, I felt moved to report that Rhoades had gone one way, Brown had gone the other and poor old Neil Berry was left with the hyphen!

Neil had the last laugh though. After a free transfer from Burnden Park, he signed for mighty Hearts and shared in all of the Jam Tarts' recent triumphs. And good luck to him!

Surprisingly, the only person who ever allowed himself to become a little irate over one of my jolly japes was Manchester City manager Billy McNeill, when I had the temerity to ever-so-gently ridicule one of his latest in a long line of Scottish-born signings.

I get along very well with Billy McNeill, but this particular morning his porridge cannot have been quite to his liking. So he did not appreciate it when I came on the air early one morning and said that I was disappointed to see that the Blues were in the process of signing goalkeeper David McKeller, because when I saw the headlines saying 'Blues sign Scotsman McKeller', I thought that they had booked the singer, Kenneth, to appear at the social club.

It was a harmless bit of fun. But Billy got his kilt in a twist and contacted the station to say that 'if Mr Eyre, with his past record of success in the game (Billy, if only you knew how that hurt!) could come up with a better suggestion, then I'd be only too pleased to consider it.'

This is what we want, a bit of reaction. But, as usual, his time would come and he was able to enjoy a spot of revenge at my expense. It would be sweet, and very, very wet.

CHAPTER 15

Unaccustomed as I am

It was recently revealed during a nationwide survey of a huge cross-section of the population that man's second biggest fear is public speaking. The greatest fear being death, although I have to say that in the case of some of the speakers I have heard, they both amount to the same thing!

I can understand the trepidation. We have all attended family weddings and squirmed with embarrassment while the best man, the bride's proud father, or indeed the groom himself, have struggled through their obligatory speeches. 'I'd like, first of all, to thank my in-laws for their gift of a beautiful perky copulator ... I mean coffee perc ...'

It is not an easy thing to do, and if a person is likely to suffer at weddings and other small family gatherings, when they are among friends (and the in-laws), then what must it be like addressing a room full of total strangers? For me, the whole phobia regarding public speaking was encapsulated by a little incident a few years ago.

It was just one little moment, over in a second, but one which had a profound effect upon me and one which I will never forget. It was a glittering Royal Variety Club Luncheon at Birmingham's Albany Hotel to present the award to Central Television's Sports

Personality of the Year, and I had been invited along as the main speaker. The room was packed with Midland-based sportsmen and showbusiness stars who mingled with the local businessmen. There were a number of main contenders for the award including athlete David Moorcroft, footballers from Aston Villa and boxer Tony Sibson, who was seated next to me on the top table.

Sibson, a very popular middleweight from Leicester, had recently returned from America, after unsuccessfully trying to take the World Middleweight title from the fearsome 'Marvellous' Marvin Hagler. The fight had been stopped in Hagler's favour, but, as usual, the British public was full of admiration for Tony, who gave such a gutsy performance against a truly great champion.

I don't know about anybody else, but I only have to see a picture of Hagler in the newspapers and my blood turns cold. The very sight of him frightens me to death. And, while I will admit that the vision of Mike Tyson in a bad mood will never find its way into a Walt Disney movie, I find the thought of Hagler a different proposition altogether. The champ from Brockton, Massachusetts, looks like one mean dude to me, and this nice lad seated next to me had recently been battling with him for 20 minutes. I was pleased to see him alive and looking quite well.

Eventually, compere Jarvis Astaire rose to his feet to introduce me and was just into his second sentence, '... we're very lucky to have him with us today, because he's a very busy ...', when Tony leaned across and whispered into my left earhole: 'I couldn't do what you're going to do now for a million pounds.'

I looked at him in genuine amazement. 'You're joking,' I said. 'You've just gone six rounds with Hagler.'

'I mean it,' he said. 'Not for a million quid.'

He did mean it too.

Different strokes for different folks. He would have

been prepared to stand and trade murderous punches with Hagler all day, but he would have turned and fled rather than speak to this audience – and I was not prepared to try to persuade him to exchange jobs with me!

An audience of over 350, gourmet food, chandeliers like Bet Lynch's earrings hanging from the ceiling, celebrities decorating every table, I had been catapulted into the international arena of public speaking with no experience of playing in the 'A' and 'B' teams, let alone the first division ... if only my rise to fame as a footballer could have been as meteoric, I would have given Bobby Moore a good jog for his money!

It was a far cry from my first public engagement in Chorley, a little pavilion on the ground where the Chorley Motors football team used to play and, indeed, where I sometimes trained during my two seasons as a player in the Northern Premier League with Chorley FC.

I was surprised to be invited. The biggest audience that I had ever spoken to at any one time was 11 – every Saturday before the game at 2.55 – and my first thought was to decline the offer politely. I finally decided to accept, however, simply because I felt that it would be the coward's way out to refuse and that I really should be able to speak to a small gathering of people for a short time without making a complete fool of myself.

I had about six weeks to prepare for the job and spent almost the whole of that time worrying about what I was actually going to say. I had attended one or two similar functions in the past and had thoroughly enjoyed them from the comfort of the audience! I had enjoyed and identified with the stories told by great sportsmen of their achievements and accomplishments during their chosen careers: winning Cup-final goals, England appearances, Test centuries, championship knockouts, match-winning tries – all great stuff.

So, with this in mind, I decided to sit down and list all of my own achievements and, to be quite honest, it did not make very good reading. Instead, I decided there and then that if I was to come through this engagement unscathed (Oh! Why did I say yes?), I would have to approach things a little differently to everybody else. I decided that I would highlight all the low-spots of what, after all, had been a fairly low-key career (I make Eddie the Eagle seem like Daley Thompson), and generally poke a bit of fun at myself. At least it would save the audience the trouble of doing it themselves later!

So, with this plan of attack now firmly in mind, I sat down and drafted out the skeleton of a script. The only thing that remained now, was the small problem of actually narrating it to a live audience. Easier done than said!

The people of Chorley were very kind; I was always very popular at the club ... when I was injured! So I just about managed to make it through the night by declining to eat the food and by taking an extra supply of my migraine tablets. I could not really determine whether the applause was out of sympathy for a lad who'd had a go, or from genuine appreciation. It was the same type of applause that I used to receive when I had been substituted as a player, I could not tell the difference then either. However, it did enable me to sit down in some degree of comfort and I was grateful for it. But, before the evening was over, I found myself agreeing to follow this triumph with another one for a football club in Longridge near Preston the following week, and at a rowing club in Northwich the week after.

This was beginning to get a little out of hand already. At Longridge, Bill Perry, who scored the winning goal in the Matthews final in 1953, was in the audience, together with current players Paul Fletcher and Peter Noble from Blackpool and ex-Liverpool star Brian Hall. I was now talking to professionals!

And rowing! What do I know about rowing except for the fact that it is the only sport, since I stopped playing football, where the participants go backwards the whole time! I had also heard that rowers have one or two strange rituals, like always patting their little cox at the end of every race! I did not much fancy that one at all, but I wanted to ask somebody connected with the sport why it was that it was always the same two teams, Oxford and Cambridge, who reach the final every single year. Is it a fix?

The success of those two dinners made me assess the situation in a completely different light. They were a little more up-market than my first one – most of the audience dipped their bread into their soup, instead of their ties! – and I had coped very well. The bookings absolutely flooded in.

With hindsight, I must have been heaven-sent for those occasions. It must have been wonderful to be able to engage a speaker who never asked for a fee. I did not realize that people actually got paid for driving hundreds of miles through the night, squirming for three hours with nerves, before speaking to two or three hundred total strangers and hopefully keeping them amused for two or three minutes. Actually, I usually speak for half an hour, but only keep them amused for two or three minutes!

I never asked for a penny. So, naturally, nobody offered it to me and I merrily accepted booking after booking all over the country. It must have cost me a fortune.

It took a chance remark at a dinner in Knutsford to bring me to my senses. The evening was an absolute sensation. The other speaker was fabulous, the comedian was marvellous and, it has to be said, I was very

111

well-received myself and, at the end of my speech, I was tickled pink to be presented with a box of Mars Bars.

Afterwards, while most people were socializing at the bar, I nipped out into the car park to put my Mars Bars into the boot of my car. They would see me nicely through a few matches in the forthcoming weeks. It was pitch dark, but I could hear the voices of one of the guests congratulating a committee member on the success of the evening.

'The football manager and the comedian were very good,' I heard him say, 'but that other speaker was absolutely sensational. Where did you find him?'

They obviously did not realize that 'the other speaker' was no more than ten yards away from them, preening himself, as he carefully placed his goodies into the car. The committee man roared with laughter and said: 'We paid the comedian a big fee, we paid the manager twice as much, but you'll never guess what we paid the lad ...' He could hardly spit it out by this time, he was almost convulsed with laughter. 'A box of Mars Bars! Honest. A box of bleedin' Mars Bars.'

As it happens, I quite like Mars Bars. I also like people laughing at me, either during the dinner, when they are supposed to, or on the football pitch, where I had become accustomed to it! But this was a different matter altogether. Something would have to be done about this.

CHAPTER 16

Let us spray

It took me quite some time to adjust to the fact that I was now being classed as an after-dinner-speaker. I still cannot equate the title with me. I much prefer to regard myself as the lad from down the road who is asked to get up and speak. But, after my appearances at just about all the top venues and for most of the top companies and organizations in the country over the years, I suppose that I will just have to start getting used to it.

There are different reasons why people agree to put themselves through the agonies of an after-dinner-speech. Obviously there is the financial aspect. For some, it is the way they earn their living, but while it is nice to have a few bob in my pocket at the end of the week, I do not do it simply for the money. Others just love to perform. They cannot wait for the meal to finish so that they can stand up and entertain, and once they are on their feet, you simply cannot get them to sit down again. Most definitely, I do not fall into this category either. I admit that I enjoy the evenings. It is great to meet old friends and former playing colleagues scattered around the country – pals that I have not seen for many years and would probably never see at all if it was not for those functions. If I could just attend them all and miss out my little bit of speaking in between, then I would be very pleased!

The real reason I do it, though, is good old-fashioned vanity, pure and simple.

I know in my heart that I would never be invited to join the England World Cup-winning team purely as a footbailer, or be guest of honour with Geoff Hurst, Tom Finney and Sir Stanley Matthews. I certainly would not find myself standing off-stage in a little room, just Bobby Moore and me, listening to the compere announce: 'Gentlemen, please be upstanding and welcome your two special guests this evening: England's World Cup-winning captain Bobby Moore and Fred Eyre.'

No! I am sure that I would never be in a position like that, simply because of my ability as a footballer.

Also, I realize that Phil Thompson, David Armstrong, Sammy Lee, Alan Warboys, Phil Neal, George Burley, Ray Kennedy and dozens more great players would never invite me to play in their testimonial games for my soccer skills. But I am the first name on their team-sheet when they come to organize their sportsmen's dinners. It is also true to say that while it is a great pity that Arsenal, Sunderland, West Brom, Aston Villa, Everton, Liverpool – in fact, about 70 of the 92 League clubs to date – never rang me to play for them and pull on one of their famous shirts, it is very flattering that they have all been anxious to sign me on as a speaker. So, I have to admit that I enjoy being there, with all of these great footballers, world-class sportsmen and top-flight entertainers, in my own right, on equal terms. After all, the old ego took quite a battering during my playing career, so it is the least I could do to let it run wild, now that I have the chance.

It got to the stage at one point, however, where I felt that I had possibly reached saturation point and did not want to overstay my welcome. Again, this was something new for me. Usually the door is held wide open while somebody else shouts '... and don't forget your boots'. So I had a quiet word with Les Dawson, another Blackley lad who hasn't done too badly for himself, and who has obviously experienced just about everything during his showbusiness career.

'Don't be so bloody daft,' he told me, straight to the point. 'You're doing great. And as long as they want you, grab it while it's there.'

I think that is the only time in my life that anybody has ever told me that I was 'doing great'. I wish that he had been one of my managers or coaches!

If it was not for sportsmen's dinners, I swear that this country would be overrun with chickens! Sometimes we have turkey or beef, although the beef is not so popular now after the Mad Cow Disease scare. Mind you, it has never affected moo! At the Wimbledon FC dinner raw meat is the order of the day, of course, but generally it is soup, chicken and apple pie.

Pork is quite popular too, except, of course, at Jewish functions. I have mixed with Jewish people for most of my business life, since the age of about 21, when I first opened my own business. At that time I coached an all-Jewish football team called Waterpark in the evenings. I am not Jewish myself (although I am saving up to be one!) and I feel that I understand the mentality of my Jewish friends and, consequently, I like them.

Jewish lads seem to be born with an inbuilt confidence in their ability, especially in business. In fact, any race that cuts a bit off the end before they know how long it is going to be is simply oozing with confidence! And their dinners are invariably huge glittering affairs that raise a lot of money for various charities.

I am asked to speak at many Jewish functions, due, I suppose, to my rapport with the lads. On one particular occasion I was asked to speak at a predominantly

Jewish golf club deep in the heart of the lovely Cheshire countryside (rather than at their regular pub, the Kosher Horses!) and I was much looking forward to it. However, just prior to the function, I had to go into hospital for a cartilage operation and so I was not sure what condition I would be in on the day. The MC for the evening was to be one of my best friends, top FIFA referee Neil Midgley, and the other speaker was Manchester City manager Billy McNeill, who I hoped had forgiven me for spoiling his breakfast the morning I discussed the merits of goalkeeper David McKeller.

Coming round from the anaesthetic, I felt a little bit woosy. My left knee was throbbing a little, and while a pain-killer put a stop to that, it could not dull the sound of Russell Grant's voice on TV-am and I half-wished that I were still on the operating table.

I had recently spoken at a dinner at the famous Winter Gardens in Blackpool for the Fylde Police. The event took place in one of the little ante-rooms, not the main theatre. When I arrived, there was a huge sign at the entrance saying 'Russell Grant on Stage' and, across it, an orange fluorescent sign bearing the words 'Tonight's show cancelled due to unforeseen circumstances'. I kid you not! I had thought it was a joke, but when I asked the commissionaire if it was true, he said it was, because they had sold only four tickets.

Obviously, under my post-operative haze, the easiest thing would have been to ask my wife to ring up and say that I was indisposed. But I did not want to let people down, so I thought that if Neil Midgley chauffeured me to and from the venue and I did not bend my leg, a cartilage operation would not be enough to keep me out of action. So with that, I changed into my brand new suit, new shirt and tie. I felt like a dummy in Burton's window with all my new gear and a stiff left leg and, while not feeling one hundred per cent, I felt well enough to get through the evening.

It was indeed a pukka do. I recognized many business faces in the audience; the chief coroner for Manchester, Leonard Gorodkin, was there (I'll be OK if I 'die' tonight); big pop impresario Danny Betesh, an old friend of mine, was also there with Stuart Diner, a well-known Manchester playboy, enjoying a wonderful evening. Neil Midgley was brilliant, he put everybody at ease with his ad-libs and general control of events and Billy McNeill also spoke very well indeed.

I have heard most of the sporting speakers, and I always enjoy hearing about their personal exploits, rather than those who follow the same path and repeat each other's 'true stories'. Billy McNeill has great presence, and a clear Scottish voice, very reminiscent of that of his great friend, ex-world champion boxer Jim Watt. He told of the time when he and his wife went on holiday with ex-Manchester United star Pat Crerand and his wife Noreen. Pat and Billy were team-mates together at Celtic, but Pat had moved to Manchester United before Billy led Celtic to that memorable European Cup triumph in Lisbon in 1967 and thus became the first ever British team to win the trophy. Pat had to wait until 12 months later, when his team beat Benfica, to become the first English team to do the job.

Some time later, the two lads decided to have their precious medals made into a necklace for their wives. One day the two girls were sunning themselves on the beach, each wearing their necklace, when a beautiful Dutch lady passing by, stopped to admire them.

'They are really beautiful,' she remarked. 'I think I will get one of those myself.'

The two girls looked at each other, smiled a little, and said as kindly as possible: 'You can't buy one of these, I'm afraid, they have got to be won.'

'Oh! I know that ... my husband has three of them!' With that, Mrs Haan, wife of Dutch international and Ajax superstar Arie Haan, continued her little stroll along the beach.

Lovely story that. Better than a dozen jokes.

The evening was turning into a great success, so much so that it was unnecessary for Neil to resort to any sympathetic remarks to the effect that I had just climbed off the operating table that morning and that I was still in great pain to get the audience on my side. He introduced me in his own inimitable style without mentioning my operation and I received a tumultuous reception before I had even said a word. This was going to be a special night!

The audience was wonderful to me – warm and spontaneous – and life was grand as I approached the middle of my speech. From the darkness, I became faintly aware of a little bit of movement, but nothing to cause me any problems I thought, until I picked him out like a moth in the spotlight, a big, plump-looking geezer with a bald head. I still did not pay much attention to him, and the audience were still laughing loudly at my last line when he lurched out from behind his table and came swaying towards me, like an MFI wardrobe!

Sometimes, in situations like this, I may make some reference to somebody wandering about, 'Is this a sponsored walk, or can we all join in?' or 'OK! Sit down now, we've all seen the suit!' but this was such a super-high-class event, that I simply decided to ignore him and allow him to go to the toilet in peace.

A few strides later and he was standing slap bang in front of me, I saw that there was a bulge under his jacket, but did not give it a thought until he snarled at me: 'You can dish it out, but you can't take it.'

With that, he produced from under his coat a soda syphon, full to the very top, and proceeded to hose me down with it, from head to foot, until every last drop had gone from the bottle.

I could not believe it. It could have been a gun. In that split-second, I knew how John Lennon must have felt. But fortunately for me, I was still alive – wet, but alive. I do not know what snapped me back to life, the deadly hush, or this idiot still leering at me from the other side of the table.

I looked down at myself. My nipples were sticking through my shirt like Ursula Andress in *Dr No*! My new suit and tie were soaked. My hair was plastered down like Max Wall's. I looked at Neil Midgley. His jaw was gaping wide open – it is the only time I have ever seen him with his mouth open and him not actually saying anything. I really had reached saturation point now!

Seconds later, all hell let loose as my assailant was led away and Neil handed me a napkin to dry myself, while the audience waited to see what was going to happen next. My mind was racing at 100 mph, my hand was shaking so much as I held the microphone that the noise of it rattling against my wedding ring was echoing around the room, out of the loudspeakers.

I gathered my thoughts and said: 'Well gentlemen, tonight is the highlight of my extinguished career. And, while I'm feeling a little put out by what's happened, you have been such a wonderful crowd that we'll row on and make the best of it.'

Naturally, they all appreciated my guts, gave me another tremendous ovation and I tried to pick up where I had left off, which was not an easy thing to do. I just wished that it had been Chris Waddle – he probably would have missed me altogether!

CHAPTER 17

An early bird breakfast

The after-dinner circuit can be very hard work – Southampton one evening, South Shields the next – and if you have to get up every morning at 6 am as I had to, then it obviously becomes even more exhausting. A good night's sleep really becomes a sweet and distant memory when you leave Bournemouth at 1 am and drive straight into the studio in Manchester five hours later, still wearing a bow tie and dinner jacket. The old dossers, who were just waking up around that time from under their cardboard duvets, thought that it was waiter service when they used to spot me coming around the corner.

My little contribution to Piccadilly Radio's Breakfast Show went on air live, every morning at 7.45. To come up with some lively, interesting and factual sporting material every single morning, when your eyes look like spit holes in the snow, and your lungs feel like a disused piano accordion from inhaling enough cigar smoke the night before to frighten the life out of a whole team of doctors from St Bartholomew's Hospital, is not an easy thing to do.

They say never work with animals and children, but at Piccadilly Dave Ward should be added to the list, if you want him to stick to the script!

Curly Shirley, as he loves to be known, is a tremendously talented radio presenter. He sends himself up mercilessly, pretending to be younger, more handsome, more virile and attractive to women than he actually is. He is easygoing and so laid back that he takes valium as a stimulant! He is a joy to work with, unless you ask him to say anything specific to lead you into your next line.

His knowledge of sport and football is so abysmal that I am surprised he never became a director! He thinks that a far post cross, is something you wear around your neck! So I was always able to have a bit of fun with him about football. Therefore when it was reported one morning that Liverpool's Kenny Dalglish had sustained a fractured cheek-bone during a game the previous evening, I decided to end my piece by making reference to his injury.

I am one of Dalglish's many admirers, both on and off the field. Even somebody like Curly Shirley, if he went to a game, would realize that he was watching a superstar in action. Even so, I must admit that I have been surprised and impressed by the way he has made the transition from player to manager, and the cool, professional and single-minded way in which he approaches the job. His handling of the media can sometimes leave a little bit to be desired, of course. In fact, with some members of the press, he is about as popular as the fan who stands on the terraces at Borussia Möenchengladbach and starts chanting 'Give us a 'B' ...' But I feel that he has seen so many managers, and players for that matter, allow themselves to be stitched up and misquoted over the years, that he had been cute enough to think to himself that he is not going to be manipulated in the same way. Consequently, he selects his words as carefully as he selects his team and, as such, is very rarely caught out.

I would not presume to call him a lifelong friend, but my dealings with him have always been first-class and he soared in my estimation not long ago, when he appeared in a testimonial match at Deepdale, for Mick Baxter, Preston North End's former centre half, who had tragically died not long previously.

It was decided that the current North End team would play a team of players selected from most of the other Lancashire clubs. Bruce Grobbelaar and Kenny came from Liverpool, Dave Watson, Kevin Ratcliffe and Trevor Steven from Everton, Leighton James from Burnley, Clayton Blackmore from Manchester United and Blackpool sent young left back Steve Morgan, a promising player who, they obviously felt, would benefit a great deal from playing alongside such great players and characters.

Bobby Charlton was the manager of the team and Wilf McGuinness and myself were the trainers. The dressing room was loud and lively, as you would expect with extroverts like Brucie and Frank Worthington, who would be stars in any company, bustling about. The only person who was totally silent was young Morgan – 19 years of age and very shy. No matter how we tried, nobody could get a peep out of him, he just seemed totally in awe of everybody around him, except me of course! And he looked as confused as a hedgehog on Bruce Forsyth's dressing table!

Grobbelaar showed Steve a trick or two. Nothing. Wilf told him a few of his jokes. Nothing – mind you, I am not surprised about that! I chatted away to him as I rubbed oil into his legs. Nothing. Then Kenny, half-dressed, quietly wandered over to his bag, took out two pairs of boots, showed them to the young lad and asked: 'Stevie, I don't play on this artificial turf very often. You've played on it before – which boots do you think I should wear?'

The boy's eyes lit up and he willingly gave the Scottish international with over a hundred caps the benefit of all of his 18-month-long football career's experience, by explaining to him just why he should wear one pair of boots instead of the other.

I was impressed. It did not take a lot, just a moment's thought. It was done without any fuss and the kid felt much better as a result. I knew, Kenny knew, and probably Stevie himself knew, that Dalglish would play brilliantly if he chose to wear a pair of Doc Marten's, but it was a nice touch all the same.

However, this particular morning, as I prepared my script, Kenny would have been in considerable pain in hospital. I confided to Dave Ward before the show that I was going to mention the Liverpool star's unfortunate accident, and, when I did, I would just like him to say one word ... nothing else at all ... just the one word 'depressed'.

'Will you do that for me, Dave?'

'No problem. You just want me to say "depressed".'

'Yes!'

The show was merrily spinning along and I was coming to the end of my spot.

'Finally, bad news for Liverpool fans. Striker Kenny Dalglish has been detained in hospital overnight, suffering from one of those fractured cheek-bones, er ...' I paused long enough for Wardy to say his one, single word, 'depressed', and then smarty pants me would top it by using the age-old joke, and retort indignantly: 'Well, he isn't very happy about it!' Boom! Boom!

Dave looked up from his turntables at the sound of his cue and cheerfully said: 'And is he very depressed about this?'

Never work with animals, children and ...!

Actually, the Breakfast Show was great fun to do. Wardy was wonderful and, in his absence, Timmy Mallett and young Andy Crane often filled in for him, before they both moved on into television.

Mallett, who has carved a niche of individuality for

123

himself on TV-am with his Wide Awake Club, possesses, to use one of his own phrases an 'utterly, utterly brilliant' brain. In fact, it is probably the only one of its kind in captivity, thank goodness! His whacky ways, incessant chatter and zany outlook on life became quite a challenge for me when we worked together in the mornings.

We would be chatting together, live on air, maybe discussing the merits of his favourite team Oxford United, and, instead of sitting opposite me like any normal presenter would do, he was tying his shoelaces, stirring his tea, combing his hair, wandering around, writing on the blackboard, and all the while talking to the listeners, with me trying my best to keep pace with him.

I am pleased that he is now quite a big star; and the same goes for Crazy Legs, as we used to call Andy Crane when he presented the show. Andy was always willing to do any little job that was asked of him. He would brew up, take me out in the studio car to football matches simply to set up my equipment. He would then spend the next 90 minutes huddled in the car listening to the radio, rather than watching the game. But he would always turn up at half time with a hot drink for me to warm the cockles of my heart.

What a good lad he is, and I knew that he was prepared to undertake all of these menial tasks because, even though he was only a youngster, he knew deep down exactly where he was going. He possesses a determined streak and was gathering as much experience as he possibly could before he made his planned assault on the big, wide, media world outside the confines of the Manchester area.

Whenever we appeared together, however, it seemed as though it was the cue for a major tragedy. It is not often while you are actually broadcasting that a little piece of paper is pushed in front of you with the instructions 'Read this out, and then get off the air' written on it. 'We have to interrupt this programme to go over to the newsroom for a newsflash.' But it happened to Andy and me so often that we seriously began to think that we were a jinx – there was the Harrods bomb disaster, the Eccles train crash (which was near to both our homes). There was even the time that Billy McNeill signed an Englishman! Crazy legs and myself invariably copped for the lot, but the experience was invaluable and it is lovely to see him handle himself so well now that he is so much in the public eye.

Andy was with me one memorable night at Gigg Lane, Bury, when The Shakers beat Stockport County 3–2. Just as we were both wrapping things up with my final analysis of the game, the producer in the studio screamed down my earphones: 'We are going to be short of material at 9.30, grab somebody for an interview.'

I needed that like David Pleat needs a tin of trophy polish, but I dashed from the press box, hoping to grab Stockport's Mickey Quinn, who I knew would always grunt a few words for me, or Dean Emmerson, a Salford lad I had just nominated as my man of the match and for whom I had predicted a bright future, or Bury's Tommy Gore, who is one of my closest friends.

Luckily, Tommy was the first person I saw and, while he was still tying his tie in front of the mirror, with his hair still straggled and soaking, zip still undone, I dragged him unceremoniously back to the press box at the other end of the main stand.

Tommy Gore and I became great pals at Wigan Athletic. We roomed together on our close-season trips abroad, and he and his wife, Janet, often go out together with Judith and me or else we will phone each other two or three times a week. Because of this, and because he is an all-round good egg, he did not deserve what I inflicted upon him this particular evening.

We were both a little breathless by the time we reached the press box – him by the exertions of the previous 90 minutes, me by the fact that I was getting old and past it! I made contact with the studio, told them that I had Tommy Gore for the interview and Andy Crane plugged me live into the show, so I could hear through my headphones exactly what the listeners at home could hear. 'That was Status Quo, and now we've just got time to go back to Gigg Lane where Fred Eyre is talking to Bury's Tommy Gore.'

I gave Tom the thumbs up, and away we went: 'Well Tommy, you certainly made hard work of it tonight.' 'Yes Fred, we were two up at half time and coasting, but full marks to Stockport for a spirited second-half comeback.'

The interview then went along the same lines as we have all heard a hundred times before, until the producer decided that we had enough to take us up to 9.30. So, while Tommy was still speaking, he said to me through my earphones: 'OK Fred, that's great. We'll just cut him off at a suitable pause in his answer, you won't hear from us again tonight. Thanks for everything, Fred. Goodnight.'

And, with that, he was gone and I was switched back to the live programme, where I could hear Tommy still talking about the game, until they cut him off at the appropriate moment and then the presenter closed the show by saying: 'Our thanks to Tommy Gore and Fred Eyre. Bury 3, Stockport County 2. The time is now 9.30.' The programme was over.

Tommy, meanwhile, totally unaware of what was happening, was still describing how the goals went in. So as not to make him feel uncomfortable, I allowed him to finish, without telling him that the last little bit actually had not been broadcast to the listeners and that the microphone was in fact now dead. It was at this point that the devil took over inside me and, as Tom finished his answer, I asked him one more question in my best radio voice and without the merest change of expression.

'Thanks Tommy. And finally, could you just tell our listeners, are you still knocking that bird off from Liverpool?'.

I can honesty say that I have never seen the colour drain from a person's face quicker than it did from Tommy Gore's that night. For a brief, horrible moment I thought that he might have a heart attack. I should never have done it. It was totally unprofessional – but it was worth it!

I could not have picked a better target. If ever there was a man who would never do such a thing it is Tommy Gore ... Janet would kill him anyway! And to see my old pal, spluttering and searching for an answer, looking helplessly at me for some assistance, is something I will never forget. Obviously I gave him no help and simply held the microphone closer to his mouth for an answer, as the records from the next show blared in my eardrums.

'Well Fred, I am from Liverpool, as you know, but I think you must be getting me mixed up with somebody else.'

I could have kept it going a little bit longer, but I could see his heart pounding under his shirt – and anyway, what sort of a friend would play a dirty, rotten trick like that?

CHAPTER 18

Fred who?

There is nothing like a good introduction and, in many cases, that is exactly what I receive as I rise to my feet, a jumble of words thrown together that constitute nothing like a good introduction.

It does not help, of course, not being a household name. So I can quite understand people not knowing much about me before I arrive anywhere, and indeed I have come to expect it. So long as they go home knowing who I am, that is the most important thing to me.

Book-signing sessions, I find, can be particularly harrowing affairs, but they are a necessary evil and go hand in glove with the publishers' wishes. Certain major bookshops in most big towns and cities specialize in 'celebrity' signing sessions and I suppose that it is very flattering to be asked to attend.

My publishers decided that such an exercise would be a good idea for me, and organized a tour of book-shops throughout the United Kingdom starting out at my local WH Smith's main branch in the city centre of Manchester. Only weeks earlier, I had managed to get through the selfsame shopping centre unscathed as Cliff Richard made a personal appearance in the same store, to autograph copies of his book *Which One is Cliff?*. I had also witnessed chaotic scenes when Terry

Wogan was there, but I could not imagine the same situation for myself and I was quite worried at the prospect of nobody actually turning up on the day.

I was unsure how I would handle a situation like that, possibly arsenic would be the order of the day. The previous Christmas had been bad enough, when I was one of the speakers at a charity dinner in Droylsden, just outside Manchester, to raise money for under-privileged children. The 300-strong audience contained showbiz stars like Bill Tarmy, Jack Duckworth from *Coronation Street*, comedian Stu Francis, Oldham Athletic manager Joe Royle and many more, but I spent the entire evening seated at the top table by myself. There was no-one even to pull my Christmas cracker with. The other speaker and comedian Bernard Manning were coming along later, after the meal, so for one reason or another, the other top table places were not occupied and I sat alone there. I found the whole scene most disconcerting and could visualize the same thing happening to me at WH Smith's in a few days' time.

Bernard Manning, contrary to what certain people say or think about him, is a wonderful person. He supports hundreds of charity events, so it was not a surprise to learn that he would be appearing with me that night, despite the fact that he had only recently incurred a personal tragedy of his own, when his famous Embassy Club had burned down. The following week he received a letter of apology from the Iranian government which simply said: 'Sorry Bernard, wrong Embassy!'

It was a personal tragedy for me also, when the old building went up in flames, because with it went one of my best photographs. Bernard had constructed a Wall of Fame in the snooker room. A collection of framed photos of some of the world's top sportsmen, each with their name and credentials proudly displayed underneath, jostled each other for space on the wall. 'Send me a photo and I'll squeeze you in,' Bernard said to me one day.

I told him that I thought that I would look a little out of place among that galaxy, but he insisted. 'The club is in Blackley and you are a Blackley lad wot done good,' he said.

It was like receiving the OBE from the Queen as far as I was concerned, so I was happy to oblige and the next time I was driving along Rochdale Road, I decided to pop in and admire myself in such distinguished company.

Sure enough, there we all were. There was a super picture of Geoff Hurst scoring a goal for England with his name underneath (West Ham United and England), Steve Davis looking interesting (world snooker champion), Nobby Stiles snarling, without his teeth (Manchester United and England), Bobby Moore with the odd hair out of place – a real collector's item that one (West Ham United and England) and a completely blank piece of paper in a frame. This should have been George Best, but he had obviously failed to turn up again! Then there was mine, and underneath Bernard had inscribed the words: 'FRED WHO?' It was very touching for me to stand there and admire it!

This particular evening at Droylsden, Bernard arrived while I was only two-thirds of the way through my speech. He burst in at the back of the auditorium with the finesse of Dave Ewing, Trevor Ford and Dave Hickson all rolled into one and shouted: 'Are you still writing those bloody awful books? He's done for writing what King Herod did for babysitting.'

And from that moment, I did have somebody to pull my Christmas cracker with, as he proceeded to take over the whole evening. I could have done with Bernard accompanying me to Smith's, this particular Saturday morning. Why should anybody want to come and see me?

Indeed, if anybody did, they had only to walk another 100 yards to my shop in John Dalton Street and I was there, all day, every single day and the nearer I got to the Arndale Centre, the more this book-signing session seemed like a very bad idea indeed.

The queue was five deep, out of the store, along The Mall and down the stairs. I thought that possibly food rationing had been brought back and that they were all queuing for bread. I was, however, relieved that my hometown people had come out to see me and it gave me the confidence to undertake the rest of the tour. Liverpool was the next stop.

The shop manager was waiting by the door as I arrived. 'Do you have many of these sessions?' I enquired.

'Oh! Yes!' he said, and proceeded to reel off a variety of showbusiness names.

'... And do you think that anybody will bother to come out in the rain, just to see me?' I asked, the old anxiety beginning to creep in again.

He sucked on his teeth, thought for a moment, and said 'Dunno, 'cos Mike McCartney only got two people here, and his brother was one of The Beatles.'

Oh, my God! I haven't even got a brother, let alone a Beatle brother. So what chance would I have? I sat there for two hours and signed three copies of the book and, on each occasion, I almost wrote another novel inside it as an inscription, simply to drag the proceedings out as long as possible.

Finally, it was time to go, thank goodness, and as I shook his hand he said: 'Well at least you got one more than Mike McCartney.'

Thank you very much. Final score: Eyre 3, McCartney 2.

St Helens was to be my final port of call. I suppose

that Jackie Collins visits Cannes, Los Angeles, Florida and New York. I visit Skelmersdale, Warrington, Runcorn and St Helens, and I must have a big following in the town, because the crowd was out in their sixes! I wonder how Mike went on in St Helens?!

I was resplendently turned out, as you would expect, just the correct amount of white cuff showing, button-down shirt, designer tie, pocket handkerchief, highly polished shoes, merrily signing copy after lovely copy, with hardly enough time to look up and smile at each recipient, but aware of everything that was going on and able to hear various snatches of conversation around me.

'What's going on over there, Elsie?'

It was vintage *Coronation Street*.

'I don't know ... I'll go and have a look.'

I carried on my good work, quietly amused, hoping possibly to snatch a glimpse of Elsie, as she investigated the fuss. I did not catch sight of her, but I heard her report back to her friend.

'Oh, it's nothing! It's just Worzel Gummidge signing copies of his book!'

Normally I would not have minded, but I was wearing my best suit at the time. The old nose may bear a slight resemblance to a carrot ... but, come on Elsie ... Worzel Gummidge! I suppose that is the price of fame.

I must say, in fairness, that it would help if just occasionally the organizers took the trouble to spell my name correctly on posters, menus and place-cards, then there would be an outside chance of the compere getting it right as well. There are only four letters to arrange in the correct order, but it is amazing the different permutations that I have had to endure. Sometimes when I arrive, it is difficult to believe that it is actually me that they are expecting and not some-body else.

I have been introduced as Fred Pye on two occasions. Fred, a very good friend of mine, is the vice-chairman of Manchester City and has been a scrap metal dealer all his working life. Now that he has moved up in the world, he prefers to say that he is in iron and steel. Fred's wife Alma does the ironing and Fred does the ... best he can!

Another time, the master of ceremonies in Northampton rose confidently to his feet and announced to the audience that it was time to introduce the main speaker of the evening. 'So it gives me great pleasure to introduce (pause ... even longer pause) my very good friend on my left.'

That was it. Thanks very much for nothing, my very good friend on my right.

Fred Ayre, Fred Air, Fred Eyres, Fred Erye, Fred Hair, Fred Astaire ... sorry that Ginger Rogers could not make it ... Red Adair (they must have thought that I had come to put the fire out) and, at a grandiose affair in Leicestershire attended by local dignitaries both male and female, the biggest insult of the lot: Fred Ayres.

One of the committee spotted me standing by the top table, bustled over, offered me a multi-jewelled hand and said: 'Mr Ayres, I'm so looking forward to hearing your wife's poetry.'

I did not bother to explain that I had never even met Pam in my life, and then proceeded to enlighten her and the audience about life at Lincoln City, Crewe Alexandra and Bradford Park Avenue.

Ladies can sometimes be a problem, especially the upper-crust variety. I am invited to speak at many mixed functions, probably because I do not swear during my speech – it might offend their husbands!

Most sporting speakers use industrial language, because in most cases, it is an integral part of their story and, at first, I tended to do the same because I

133

thought that it was the accepted thing to do. One evening in Glossop Harry Godwin was in the audience. He was the scout who had originally signed me as a bright-eyed 15-year-old for Manchester City and he came over to speak to me at the end of the evening and complimented me on the quality of my speech. 'I didn't think it was possible for one of my boys to stand up and speak like that.'

'Thanks, Harry,' I replied. That was years before Frank Bruno had even thought of the phrase. I was obviously years ahead of my time.

'But if you don't mind me saying so, I don't think that you should use any bad language at all. Leave that to the others. Be the odd one out, because in your bow tie, with your nice face (his eyes obviously weren't what they used to be!) and your freckles, up there in the spotlight, you just haven't got a swearing face.'

At that moment I had a blushing face. I had not blushed or felt flustered for years. Usually, I can cope with most things quite comfortably, but Harry had struck a nerve and I felt like Mavis Wilton standing there in front of him, inwardly squirming and writhing with embarrassment, as he smiled an apologetic, schoolmasterly smile. From that moment, I decided that, no matter how downmarket the venue, how rough the clientele, I would not swear. Even if they had tattoos that were spelt incorrectly, even if they used a pig on the bar as an air freshener, I vowed that I would not resort to using bad language, and I have not done so from that evening onwards.

Not that cursing bothers me at all. Wilf McGuinness, the extrovert former manager of Manchester United, just loves to stand up and tell his stories about the good old days of Duncan Edwards and the Busby Babes. Wilf had just broken into United's first team prior to the horrific Munich Air Disaster, and only missed the fateful trip to Belgrade because he was recovering from a cartilage operation. The pre-Munich Reds, as well as being marvellous young footballers, were also a bunch of fun-loving lads. Wilf always enjoys recounting tales of their escapades, and he liberally sprinkles his anecdotes with a few adjectives that are not to be found in any guide to correct speech.

Wilf is an old (bald!) friend and, one evening, he asked me if I felt that he swore too much during his speech. Now when Wilf gets excited, recalling those great players from yesteryear, he becomes a cross between Magnus Pyke and Bill and Ben the Flowerpot Men, arms and legs fly all over the place like an inside forward who has just been hit by a Tommy Smith tackle. Naturally, in the heat of battle, naughty words are tossed in at random; he even breaks words up to insert one. So I had to be truthful and say that I did think that he tended to overdo it a little bit.

'You're right,' he said. 'From now on, I'm going to cut it out altogether, just like you.'

Great! I would look forward to hearing it. I did not work with him for about six weeks but, at our next function together, he proudly announced that he had cracked it and said that he no longer used a single expletive during his entire speech. I was impressed – very professional. I was looking forward to hearing the new Wilf!

I spoke first. It was a lovely audience, a nice room, the microphone worked, which in itself made a pleasant change, and the scene was set for Wilf. He would have no problem. It was already a super evening.

He started off in his usual aggressive way with a brief little description of his career. '... and although we played in seven semi-final games, in an 18-month spell, we didn't win 'ucking one of them.'

The crowd roared with laughter, as they always do at this point, and Wilf looked at me for approval of his new image. I was astonished and just about managed to raise a thumb to indicate that the removal of one single letter had made all the difference. I did not want to destroy his confidence.

The audience loved it. "Ucking little Nobby Stiles ... Pat Crerand's so 'ucking slow ... George Best didn't 'ucking well turn up.'

He 'ucked his way through for 35 hilarious minutes and I was in absolute hysterics, not at his script, which I had heard many times before, but at the ludicrous situation. As he sat down to a wonderful reception, he turned to me and said: 'Well, what do you think?'

'Wilf,' I replied. 'That was 'ucking great.'

'Yes,' he nodded, seriously for a moment. 'I feel much better about it myself, because, really, there is no need for all of that bad language!'

Generally speaking, I find that the ladies in the audience are great, often more receptive than the men. They have come out to enjoy themselves and generally do their best to join in. However, I rarely take Judith along – not many men take their wives to work with them. But she really spoilt things for herself when I took her out a few years ago and, as we closed the front door behind us, she blinked in the sunlight and enquired: 'Where are all the trams?' She really knows how to upset me that girl!

It is the female guests on the top table who cause me the most pain. Usually it is the chairman's wife, the Lady Mayoress or one of the all fur coat and no knickers brigade, who are really as rough as I am, but have married into a slightly higher social situation and struggle to keep up with it. I chuckle to myself when I see them jangle their jewellery to the audience as they are introduced when, only minutes earlier, I have seen them sneak behind the curtains, take their shoes off and have a crafty drag on a Woodbine.

At one function in south Yorkshire, the Lord Mayor was greeting the guests by the door as we arrived, with a lighted fag secreted up the baggy left sleeve of his robe, while he shook hands with his right hand. A glass of water, a tube of Savlon and a portable sewing kit were needed before we could actually get the event under way, after he had set fire to himself.

After that enlightening experience, I should have known that this particular evening would be one to remember. The whole event was sponsored by a multi-national company based in London, and I was seated next to the wife of the managing director, who I watched perform her regal duties very well indeed – mingling with the guests, asking them questions, not listening to their answers and generally sweeping majestically around the room with an air of confidence that can only come from being the boss's missus. I watched her flutter around, knowing that, eventually, she would have to finish up with me, because I was the main guest, and I knew that I would be included on her list of duties.

I saw her glance at my place-card to familiarize herself with my name. She had obviously been the wife of a managing director for a long time and knew all of the tricks. She then took a deep breath and said to herself: 'Well girl, you can't put it off any longer. You'll have to go and earn your fur coat and XJS and make conversation with this bit of rough from the north of England.'

Her accent was cut glass, even though she told me that she was originally from Nottingham. Sex, for her, was definitely what potatoes come in!

'Fred! A good, solid, typically English name. Stout and reliable.' She had succeeded in ascending one nostril already and would undoubtedly get up the other one before very long. 'Do they actually call you Fred, or do they call you Frederick?'

She had done it, she was up to the bridge of my nose in record time, but I showed remarkable restraint.

'Well,' I replied quietly, 'I was christened Frederick, but everybody calls me Fred.'

'I,' she announced grandly, 'will call you Frederick ... Frederick the Great.'

She would have to be straightened out rapido, and I affected the broadest Lancashire accent possible which made Albert Tatlock sound like Alistair Burnett, and replied: 'Yer know luv, that's just what me Mam used to say to me, when she wanted me to shift the ashes in the morning.'

She looked at me like Max Bygraves trying to remember the rules to *Family Fortunes*. She had obviously never heard of such a thing. Judging by her fingernails, she had never even put the kettle on, let alone cleared out the fire grate or brought the coal in from the back yard. She obviously thought that her hubby had made a drastic mistake with his choice of speaker but, as the event wore on, she began to realize that the success of the evening and, possibly, with it, her husband's standing in the company, in front of all of his top clients, could well depend on me ... this uncouth football chappie.

There were diamond necklaces, houses in the country, and children's school fees at stake here. She decided she had better start talking to me again. Another glance at my place-card. 'Fred ... erick, a wonderful city Nottingham, don't you think?'

I am really an old softie at heart, so I thought I would give her another chance. 'Yes,' I replied, through a mouthful of profiterole. 'Some great players in Nottingham.'

Again, I received the same blank look; we were obviously from totally different worlds and at that moment I felt sorry for her, trying so desperately hard to bring herself down to my level, and I made a little effort ... not much admittedly ... to keep the conversation going along the same lines.

'Peter Shilton,' I said.

'Maybe later, with the port,' she replied sweetly.

She thought that I was offering her a piece of stilton!

At that point, I retired gracefully from the conversation and continued to do battle with my profiteroles – they too looked nice and sweet on the outside but like her, there was nothing to them really, once you actually got your teeth into them.

CHAPTER 19

The comedians

One of the benefits of working the after-dinner circuit has been the opportunity to perform alongside top-class entertainers and to be able to see at close quarters just what goes into making people laugh. American comedian Woody Allen says that humour is a very serious business and, like most other people, I had a preconceived idea that comics, by virtue of the very nature of their business, were all hard-bitten professionals, real tough-nuts who could look after themselves verbally, or physically for that matter, because their experiences of performing in dingy little clubs up and down the country had forced them to be that way.

One night, I was working with impressionist Paul Melba in Ipswich when somebody had the temerity to heckle him from the audience. He silenced his assailant with a quick piece of repartee, and then followed it up by enquiring rather menacingly: 'Do you want to quit now ... or should I commence the verbal surgery?' He meant it too, and the smart alec wisely called it a draw.

Comics are a tough breed of course, because they have had to learn how to cope with concert secretaries who announce the sad death of one of the club members, and then immediately introduce the comedian. They have learned how to continue their act on automatic pilot on those occasions when the audience has not listened, nor laughed at one of the jokes. They cope with other entertainers thieving their acts; they learn how to change into a tuxedo in the gravel car park in the pouring rain; they have come to terms with the problems of trying to make people laugh in places where domino games often go into injury time, where they have plasma, as well as whisky, in the optics and where the attitude of the audience often is, 'never leave a "turn" unstoned!'

They learn to die with dignity. 'I don't mind dying occasionally Fred, so long as the funeral is expensive,' a top comic once told me. Almost without exception, the comedians I have worked with have been very kind to me and have gone out of their way to pass on little tips that they have picked up along their route to the top.

'Have the nerve to pause for an extra second here, it's not easy, but Jack Benny used to do it for minutes on end. Try it.' I did. That extra second seemed like a lifetime, but they were right. In fact, the pauses are probably now the most interesting parts of my speech!

'You're rushing that line far too much. Slow down.' I did, and they were right again.

'Tag this little bit of nonsense onto the end of that bit and you'll get a double laugh. I guarantee it.' I did, and they were spot on once again.

In fact, every single piece of advice that the professionals have given me has proved to be correct. But, in the case of Johnny Kennedy, actions spoke louder than words. JK hosts a very popular radio show on Liverpool's local radio station, Radio City, but for many years worked the clubs up and down the country, as a stand-up comedian. We were in Congleton and he pointed to my notes on the table and said: 'You don't need those ... rip them up.'

My God! The very thought of my notes not being there, right under my nose, brought me out in a cold sweat. 'You never look at them,' he insisted, 'and anyway it's not professional.' He knew exactly where to hurt me the most. 'Rip them up.'

I had to agree that I did not consult my notes at all; I also had to agree that possibly it was not totally professional either, but I felt that it was a darn sight more professional than forgetting the whole lot. They were like a crutch, an insurance policy, and I was frightened to stand up without them. So I told him that I could not cope without them.

'Rip 'em up!' he growled and, with that, reached across me, gathered up my precious notes and tore them into little pieces. I was horrified, but there was nothing I could do, and I have never bothered sticking them back together after I proved I could get through that night without them.

Jim Bowen showed his professionalism at a function in Ipswich when, just as he was about to speak, the electricity went off. Microphone, lights – the lot – were all out and yet he performed his entire act by shouting at the top of his voice to the audience, who were sitting, laughing by candlelight.

Super! Smashing! What a great crowd!

Thank goodness it did not happen 15 minutes earlier, while I was on.

I appeared one evening with Mick Miller (he of the pink crash helmet!). After he had finished his brilliant act, a member of the audience enquired about his availability to perform at the local amateur rugby club in Wigan and asked how much it would cost for his services. Mick told him his fee and the man replied: 'Nay, Mick! Remember, they're only th'amateurs tha' knows.'

To which Mick replied: '... and if I do the job for nowt, I'll be an amateur as well, won't I?'

I must remember that one the next time that I am put on the spot like that, because free functions can sometimes be a problem. Most of the lads try to do their share of charity work and they usually do it with the minimum of fuss and publicity. Sometimes they accept the fee and then, during the inevitable auction, buy something that they do not really need for an outrageous price. So they may well have done the job for nothing and then also chipped something extra into the kitty for good measure.

Sometimes though, people are never satisfied. Neil Midgley and I spoke at a huge charity affair one evening, with a couple of really big stars topping the bill. The event raised thousands of pounds for a well-known children's charity. Neil's expertise with the auction had raised the total even higher and, after a very hard night's graft, we both slumped back in our seats at the end of the evening, bathed in sweat and totally exhausted by our efforts. It was all worthwhile though, because we felt that the money was going to a good cause and we had both agreed privately that when we eventually received our fee we would donate it to such a worthy charity. Then the secretary of the committee came over and said, with the subtlety of a steam-roller: 'Thank you both, gentlemen, for your superhuman efforts this evening. Wonderful, absolutely wonderful. Now tell me. How much do the children owe you?'

Isn't that dreadful? He, of course, knew exactly what he was doing and I did not like it at all. At least Dick Turpin wore a mask.

There are occasions, however, when good, honest, hardworking folk can ruin things, with all the best intentions and with the best will in the world. This particular evening I was just a few miles outside Wolverhampton, helping to raise money for specialist equipment required to assist physically handicapped people. The handicapped often need special machinery simply to cope with their everyday needs.

As a great evening drew to a close, the organizer, a local man with a heart of gold who had worked for months to put the evening together, felt that it was his duty to bring proceedings to a satisfactory conclusion, even though it was obvious that he had never even held a microphone before, let alone spoken into one. He bounced up onto the stage, hoping that bravado would make up for a certain lack of expertise and, after blowing two or three times into the microphone and deafening everybody in the place, he said in a rich Black Country accent that I have not heard since they closed the Crossroads Motel: 'Is this thing on, Cloive?'

Clive assured him that we could indeed all hear him loud and clear ... definitely loud! And he was away.

'We've had a crackin' noight tonight, with a crackin' speaker. Oi'm sure yow'll all agree with me about that and we've roised a tremendous amount of money and it's all due to your generositeee. So all that remains now is for me to present the cheque.' He was doing well up until this point. 'So if I could just ask the head cripple to come up, ploise, to receive it.'

There is definitely no answer to that. But the mind goes blank sometimes when you find yourself in a position that you are not used to – it used to happen to me every time I ventured into the opposing penalty area! After all, he had proved that he cared enough about the problems faced by the handicapped to put on the dinner in the first place. He was prepared to do all the chasing about, selling tickets, booking caterers and speakers, so he was entitled to one slip of the tongue at the very end. The important thing was that these people now have the use of the complicated and expensive pieces of machinery which can help make their lives a little easier, and he was the man responsible for this. And that is what it is all about.

CHAPTER 20

Close circuit

There is never an evening goes by without somebody asking me the same question: 'Do you still get nervous before you stand up to speak?'

I always answer truthfully and admit that I do, and qualify this by saying: 'Anybody who tells you that they are not nervous is either telling lies or they are Bob Monkhouse.'

I use Monkhouse as an example, because to me he always appears to be the ultimate professional, completely in control and on top of every job that he takes on, and I simply could not imagine him suffering from an attack of nerves or stage fright. He has been doing his job, at the very top of his profession, for so long that, just like my old pal Natty in Hollywood, I am sure that, on stage, he could cope with just about anything that comes his way with style and panache.

Of course, nothing comes easy. Years of hardbitten experience and many hours of painstaking preparation and study have gone into making Bob Monkhouse what he is today – plus a filing cabinet in his brain marked 'ad-libs for all occasions'. We see a beautiful, serene swan gliding effortlessly across the pond. What we do not see is a little pair of webbed feet, working like the clappers, keeping the whole thing afloat. It is the same with Bob Monkhouse, Bruce Forsyth and all the other top-liners: it is definitely a lot more difficult than it looks.

I have admired Monkhouse's talent for many years, but until recently I had never met him. I even spent an evening at a club in Manchester scrutinizing his act and not listening to a single joke. I simply studied his timing, watched him manipulate his audience, saw how he moved about the stage and marvelled at the way in which he managed to wring every last drop of entertainment possible out of every movement. I learned a great deal that night. I must have been the only person in the room not to laugh – I was too busy studying to enjoy myself!

I was delighted to learn, some months later, that he was to be the top speaker at a gala awards dinner in London. I had been the speaker at the same event the previous year so, when I arrived and saw Bob already seated at the top table making a few notes, I felt that, with my vast experience in these matters, I had a legitimate reason to go over and introduce myself and possibly give him a few tips about the job in hand. After all, no two dinners are the same, and maybe there would be a little something I could possibly help him with, having already done the job myself.

He was charming; but what pleased me more than anything was that he seemed a little nervous as he jotted little reminders down on his programme. He swallowed a large whisky before he went on stage and had another one strategically placed for a quick nip, possibly to be drunk during his act. This perked me up no end, showing me that even the greats go through the same agonies as I do before they actually stand up and entertain.

I will admit that the whisky came as a bit of a surprise, one shot would put me on my back for a week, but it obviously puts Bob on his mettle – just like the great American comedian WC Fields. He always used to have a couple of scotches before every performance. One night he offered his guest star a quick slug, but the guest refused to drink before a performance: 'You mean to tell me that you're going out there alone?' asked an incredulous Bill.

Indeed, I am sure that if stars like Bob, Brucie and Ken Dodd did not suffer from a touch of nerves, their performances would not be of the high standard that we have come to expect from them over the years.

Even the great Sir Stanley Matthews used to be physically sick before every game ... the opposing left back used to feel the same way afterwards! He once told me that he did not feel 'just right' if he did not spend those few moments in private at 2.50 every Saturday afternoon.

Stanley Matthews is, of course, one of the greatest footballers of all time. Towards the end of an unparalleled career in the game, he became football's first knight and, after he retired, he set off around the world spreading the gospel of the game that he played professionally until just after his 50th birthday. He became a soccer missionary in places as various as Soweto in South Africa, Malta and Canada, coaching and coaxing youngsters the whole time, and bringing football into the lives of kids who had rarely, if ever, seen a top-class game.

To celebrate his 70th birthday, a group of his admirers were flying him from his home in Burlington, Ontario, for a gala dinner in Blackpool, the scene of many of his great triumphs. It promised to be a wonderful night of football nostalgia. Many of Stan's great playing colleagues from the past, from Blackpool and England, had been rounded up and the guest list read like a footballers' who's who: Jimmy Mullen, George Hardwick, Johnny Carey, Neil Franklin, John Charles, Jackie Mudie, Jackie Milburn, Tom Finney – the list was endless. I felt very honoured to be invited as the guest speaker. Putting me in a room with that lot was like locking Lou Macari in a betting shop! I was in my element, and it turned out to be a truly memorable evening.

Sir Stan seems genuinely shy. Obviously he knows how great a footballer he was, but he is reluctant to discuss his own achievements. I found him to be extremely pleasant company, with a warm personality and a soft voice that still shows traces of a Potteries accent, despite his globe-trotting existence. It was hard to imagine, as I chatted the evening away with him, that it was the same man that I had queued for hours to watch as a youngster, so many times at Maine Road, whenever Blackpool played Manchester City.

Two or three years later I was engaged to speak at Keele University for the ex-Stoke City and Port Vale Players' Association Dinner – another event that I was looking forward to, because the audience would again be made up of former players and their guests so I would be surrounded by footballers and therefore in good company.

I arrived alone and wandered into the huge baronial library that was being used as a reception area for the evening. The room was a sea of familiar faces. Alan Hudson was there and Mel Machin, but it was Sir Stan who spotted me first. He was standing by a huge open fireplace but, as soon as he saw me, he jinked his way through the crowd, as if he were weaving his way through a maze of defenders along the right touchline, and came towards me with his hand outstretched.

'Fred,' he said. 'I don't know if you remember me, but you spoke at my dinner in Blackpool.'

I am not joking!

'I don't know if you remember me'! Stanley Matthews actually said that to me ... but he meant it. That is the type of unassuming man that he is. I was tempted to reply that perhaps the face looked a little familiar, but I was too shocked to make a joke about it.

Ventriloquist Neville King was the other 'speaker' that night. He employs a number of dummies (like most football chairmen really!) but his most famous is his drunken old man, with whom, invariably, he does battle, verbally and physically, in a riotous routine where the two of them eventually end up in a tangled heap on the floor.

I had spoken first, everything was great, and I was looking forward to Neville's act. He was seated next to me, with the old man on his knee ready for action, but the raffle and the auction of an autographed Stanley Matthews tie was taking a little longer than anticipated.

'Get me on,' I heard the old man say.

'I can't get you on yet, they're still doing the raffle,' Neville replied.

'Sod the raffle, get me on now, it's getting late.'

I chanced a sly glance and saw that Neville was trying to reason with the dummy.

'I can't interrupt him just like that.' Neville caught my eye, shook his head wearily and said: 'He's getting a bit agitated, he thinks it's a bit late.'

I looked at my watch and replied: 'Well, he's right, it is 11.15.'

I'm now agreeing with a bloody dummy!

Neville did not come out of character for a second, he was preparing himself for his performance and, when he was finally introduced, he was absolutely sensational. He brought the house down, with Sir Stan leading the applause. The bigger the star, the nicer they are. That is what I have always found and, whenever I have been fortunate enough to meet Sir Stan, Sir Matt, Tom Finney, Bill Shankly, Bert Trautmann, Billy Wright, Denis Law, Peter Doherty and many more of football's true greats, I have never been disappointed.

149

It is a pity that one or two of the younger players today do not conduct themselves in public in the same way. I was the speaker, with comedian Norman Collier, at the Arsenal Players' League Championship Dinner, held at the Holiday Inn, Swiss Cottage – the very hotel that I had stayed in the fateful night of Judith's accident, when the entire Metropolitan police force was out looking for me.

It was the first time that I had been back to the place since then, and I felt uneasy as I registered at reception, hoping that they would not allocate me to the same room. It was another magic evening, for me at least. Arsenal, as well as having good players in their team, have a group of lads who are gentlemen and fine ambassadors for the game, their club and themselves. Unfortunately, this evening proved that they also have one or two in their ranks who, in my opinion, are not.

Paul Davis, Lee Dixon, Tony Adams, Alan Smith, Brian Marwood, David Rocastle, Michael Thomas, John Lukic and Perry Groves all looked immaculately turned out in their club blazers and ties. Sadly, after a few drinks, a couple of the lads looked like latter-day Freddie Frinton's with their jackets and ties all over the place.

Fortunately their behaviour did not interfere with my speech at all, and I was given a tremendous reception. But, by the time that poor Norman Collier was ready to start his act, the affair had turned into such a fiasco that Norman was unable to complete his act. He had to keep his famous chicken in the deep freeze!

The newspapers, of course, got hold of the story and the players concerned were hauled up before manager George Graham the following week to explain their side of a debacle that certainly did not do anybody any favours.

It is only a pity that the players in question were not at Highbury with me a couple of weeks prior to that event, when I was the speaker, along with TV prankster Jeremy Beadle, at a function to raise money for a charity spearheaded by Ray Kennedy, a super player who has now been struck down by Parkinson's Disease. Kennedy wore the same red Gunners' jersey with dignity and pride, and his ability won him 17 England caps and it would have been a chastening experience for those silly young players to have been present that night and seen Ray struggling a bit. It might well have brought them to their senses a lot quicker than a dozen lectures from George Graham. It certainly would have fully illustrated to them just how short and precarious the life of a professional footballer really is, and ensured that they would not abuse the privilege.

The club had booked me into an hotel so that I could relax for the afternoon before the main event, which was to be held in the new executive suite at the ground. But the traffic was so horrendous on the M1 that even the lorry carrying more cones could not get through! So I only managed to arrive at Highbury at the same time as the guests.

As I nosed my way through the streets of Islington towards the famous North Bank, the Rollers and BMWs were bumper to bumper. The diamonds sparkled from the ladies and cigars looked like telegraph poles jutting from the lips of the menfolk. It was certainly going to be an executive evening I thought, as I set about finding somewhere to change from my tracksuit into my dinner suit down some dark alleyway near the ground. Fortunately, no local resident saw me and mistook me for a flasher, or believed that Sammy Nelson had returned to the club!

Sammy is a great character, an Irish international who served Arsenal for 11 seasons and won over 50 caps for Northern Ireland in the process. Apart from the quality of his performances in the Number 3 shirt, he is fondly remembered for baring his bum to the crowd after scoring a goal during a game where the fans had given him a little bit of abuse. I had not seen him since he called at our house *en route* to a game at Liverpool one snowy night and sampled my wife's home-made Lancashire hot-pot. He's never been heard of since. Maybe he did not like her dumplings!

The doorman at Highbury was a kindly soul and, while the guests were filing into the executive suite behind the goals, he opened up the main entrance to the ground, unlocked the first-team dressing room and allowed me to change in style. Highbury is a magnificent ground with marble halls, a bust of Herbert Chapman and huge dressing rooms the size of an average dance hall, with underground central heating. What I would have given to have played for a club like Arsenal! After I had changed into my penguin suit, I was tempted to shoot off down the tunnel on to the pitch rather than make my way around the ground to the function room.

'Thanks a lot, pal,' I said as I passed the doorman.

'It's OK, mate' he replied in a voice like Max Miller. 'You're a lucky bugger going in there,' he said, pointing in the direction of the luxury suite. 'I've just seen the great Ted Drake go in there.'

They love their heroes at Arsenal.

Drake was a bustling goalscoring centre forward who once scored seven goals in one game for the club against Aston Villa in 1935 and, although into his 70s, he had come along from his home in south London to add to Ray Kennedy's night. Goalkeeper Jack Kelsey was there too. He donated Alfredo di Stefano's Spanish international jersey towards Ray's fund and the entire double-winning team turned up to help their old mate, as Bob Wilson, compere for the evening, got things underway.

It was touching to see how they all rallied around. Liam Brady bid an absolute fortune for an old Arsenal team photograph, as Jeremy Beadle frightened the whole room into spending money. Charlie George did the same for another prize and, finally, Frank McLintock drew my raffle ticket out for a monster JVC contraption that was probably the first piece of machinery of its kind. Judith and the kids will not even let me use the remote control on our TV set, let alone handle something as modern as this. So I donated it back, and Sammy Nelson paid nearly a thousand pounds for it two minutes later.

'What is it?' Sammy asked me afterwards. He had bared his wallet this time, not his bum, for Ray Kennedy's benefit and he did not even know what he had bought. Those are good lads.

People who think that, for footballers, life is just take, take, take should have been there that night to see what Bob Wilson, Frank McLintock and the Arsenal supporters did for Ray Kennedy. It was marvellous, a credit to everybody. McLintock it was who spent something like 20 minutes simply reeling off all the honours that Kennedy had won throughout his career. It seemed as though he managed to win just about everything except the George Cross – although he did convert a few of those in his time at Highbury when little Armstrong was on the wing!

All in all, it was not a bad effort from a lad who was released as a kid by Port Vale and moved back to his native north-east to work in a sweet factory before The Gunners gave him a second chance. I sincerely hope that the money raised that night goes some way towards helping him cope with his terrible and unfortunate illness, and gives him a third chance to prove what he can do.

CHAPTER 21

International cabaret

Judith was catching on fast. I could hear her speaking on the telephone downstairs and I liked what I was hearing. 'If he is going to speak in Dubai, he will want an international cap, that's for sure.' I was very impressed.

It was Gary Owen, the former Manchester City and West Brom midfield player, enquiring if I could accompany him to the United Arab Emirates to speak at two functions sponsored by Amstel, a big company out there, who, among other things, import beer.

Gary retired from football at a comparatively early age and is now a dealer in fine art. He knows a thing or two about international caps as well, because he was, at one stage during his career, the holder of a record number of Under-21 caps. He accumulated 22 in all, but unfortunately he was not at the front of the queue when the full caps were being handed out. So, like Steve Perryman of Spurs who has played almost as many games for the Under 21s as Gary, he was never able to make the final transition into the full England team. Sad really, although Steve did manage one token appearance in what was essentially a 'B' international in Iceland during Ron Greenwood's reign as England manager.

I told Gary that, for my trip to the UAE, a blue

velvet cap would do me nicely. I like Bobby Vinton! And it had to have a gold tassel, of course, and, instead of the three lions, I wanted a knife, a fork and a spoon. Very tasteful! After all, I was after-dinner speaking for my country.

The thought of speaking to an audience on the other side of the world had never entered my head. People have enough trouble trying to understand me in England, so what chance would the Arabs have? First-class travel, a fine hotel, one of the top ten in the world, and a chauffeur-driven limousine at my disposal 24 hours a day, however, quickly brought me around to their way of thinking and, in no time, after a luxurious flight, Gary and I found ourselves comfortably reclining in the back seat of the car, while our driver, Jaffa the Gaffer, ferried us around the bustling streets of Dubai.

I was only vaguely aware of the different customs and cultures in that part of the world. I had heard that beer was very expensive ... 20 lashes a pint! And that if a man commits adultery, he gets stoned, in contrast to our country where it is usually the other way round!

I was aware, however, of the feeling of opulence in the area. The ex-pats who live there agreed that they had found little difficulty adjusting to their new life-styles. Obviously, massive salaries made any minor irritations a little easier for them to bear.

The first culture shock for Gary and me came as we drove through the back streets of the town and witnessed the bizarre sight of a man having his hand stitched back on to his wrist. 'What's that all about, Jaff?' we asked.

'He must have won his appeal, sir,' replied Jaffa nonchalantly.

My first speaking engagement, at the Passport Club, was a very intimate and enjoyable dinner for British people only. But the next function that I attended, at the swish Golf and Country Club out in the desert, was a very grand affair, with the vast audience made up of a cross-section of different cultures. The main speaker for the evening was the notorious Cynthia Payne, who was reportedly being paid a colossal amount of money for her appearance.

Two major films had been based on her life, with Julie Walters and Emily Lloyd each starring as the Cynthia character, and she had become famous the world over for her lunchtime activities in south London. So, under the circumstances, I was quite happy that she was regarded as the main speaker. Madam Cyn, of course, is the lady from Streatham who organized parties for businessmen with her 'girls' ensuring that the lunchtimes were a success and she even accepted luncheon vouchers for the services provided ... we never got that at the UCP on Oxford Road!

I must admit, that I was quite looking forward to listening to her speech. I like speeches that are educational, and I thought that possibly I might learn something ... from a purely professional angle of course! Besides, I still had a few luncheon vouchers left over, so they might come in useful! Furthermore, it would be a pleasant change for me – a new departure from the various sportsmen and showbiz personalities that I usually listen to.

I was not wrong.

I did not really know what to expect. I had not analyzed the situation before I arrived at the club, but really I should not have been surprised at the outcome. Freddie Trueman is invited to functions to speak about cricket. Neil Midgley is expected to discuss refereeing. I am invited along because the audience want to hear what a bad footballer I was. Denis Law, Trevor Brooking, Alan Mullery and all the other great players are invited because that is what they were ... great players. Cliff Morgan speaks about rugby, Dickie Bird talks about umpiring, and David Pleat is also invited to speak at dinners for some reason. So really, when all things are taken into account, there is only one thing that Madam Cyn is going to talk about when she is introduced, and it is not going to be the ramifications of the internal combustion engine or Einstein's Theory of Relativity. She is going to talk about her specialist subject, the thing that she knows the best of all. Fair enough. But I do not think that I or the rest of the audience (or, indeed, the members of the Dubai Ladies' Luncheon Club the very next afternoon) were quite prepared for her to go into such graphic detail of her former professional life.

Indeed, I have been told that many a disc was slipped the night after she had spoken at the luncheon club when some of the members tried to demonstrate to their husbands one or two of the things that they had learned earlier in the day.

She certainly had some bottle – that I will give her credit for. I simply sat back and let the evening wash over me towards the end, when she threw herself at the mercy of the audience by inviting everybody to join in a question and answer session. It was a somewhat different form of group therapy to that which had been discussed a little while earlier.

To be fair, she never ducked a single question, no matter how personal. And to see this tiny little woman, not exactly in the first flush of youth, standing there, taking on all-comers, some in a really angry state of mind, as they gave vent to their feelings on the subject, just proved what a tough little cookie she must have been when she was in her prime. I would not have liked to have kicked my ball into her garden and crushed her lupins when I was a kid, I can assure you of that!

I have to say that, for Cyn, the evening was not a cultural success. Joan Bakewell she most definitely is not but, by all accounts, it was a financial success. I ate

157

breakfast with her the following morning and, by the way she tackled that sausage, I was glad that I never lived in Streatham! I gently suggested to her that if she could possibly inject a little more humour into the proceedings, then maybe she would not antagonize quite so many of the straight-laced members of the audience, as she had obviously done the previous evening.

She said that she would give the matter a bit of 'fort' – Angela Rippon she is not either! And off she toddled, to educate the ladies at their luncheon club. From what I gather, the husbands offered to have a whip-round to pay for her to make a return visit or, more likely, have a whip-round when she actually got there!

Cynthia is not the first personality in my experience who has found the transition into after-dinner speaking a somewhat painful experience. Showbusiness entertainers, steeped in the true tradition of keeping an audience either interested or amused – preferably both, of course – have no problem. Sportsmen, too, generally speaking, have little trouble bridging the gap. But ordinary, everyday folk who, by some quirk of fate or by the unusual nature of their occupation, find themselves in the public eye, are not slow to accept the offers to speak publicly about their exploits, but on the occasions that they have worked with me, have often seemed to experience great difficulty in actually putting it across.

Ted Moult was one. He suffered excruciating agonies as he laboured through his speech one evening in Wilmslow. Ted was a farmer, but, due to a little bit of exposure on radio and TV, had suddenly become a personality in his own right, accepting bookings to appear in pantomime with former Miss World Ann Sydney and doing the speaking rounds with, if that evening's offering was anything to go by, very little of interest to talk about.

It was very sad when it was reported that Ted had committed suicide not long after that appearance at Wilmslow. His speech was not that bad! He just seemed to me to be a very nice, gentle, sensitive man who had suddenly been thrust into the spotlight and obviously found it a much different world to agriculture, where you just have to milk cows, you do not have to make them laugh.

I also spoke on one occasion with Fred Dibnah, at a huge dinner at the Leyland Motor factory just outside Preston. Fred is the steeplejack from Bolton who found fame when he appeared in a TV advertisement enjoying a pint of beer while toppling a gigantic chimney. As a reward for a job well done, Fred pushed back his grimy cap and, with a toothy grin showed the viewer just how much he loved his pint of ale, as the huge chimney crumbled in the background. It was a clever piece of television, brought to life by Fred's expressive face. It captured the imagination of the public and catapulted Fred into the category of 'personality' and brought with it the inevitable invitations to speak publicly about his unusual lifestyle.

Football legend Tom Finney, Ireland manager Billy Bingham and Liverpool's Mark Lawrenson were among the top-table guests, as Fred, in his dinner-suit and bow tie, suddenly thrust his now famous grubby old cap onto his head and he rose to his feet. He received a warm ovation and opened his speech to the audience of over 300 in his broad Lancastrian accent by saying: 'Not a reet lot of interesting things happen to me, stuck up on top of a chimney.'

We all laughed. It was not a bad opening line. But unfortunately, Fred then proceeded to prove just that, to such a degree that, after a few minutes, people were walking around, standing about in groups chatting and, believe it or not, playing cards on one table on my right-hand side, as Fred prattled on, and on ... and on.

159

I suppose a chimney is a chimney really. Like one player said, when he declined the chance to visit the Great Wall of China during West Bromwich Albion's tour of the Far East: 'When you've seen one wall, you've seen them all!'

I much prefer manager Ron Atkinson's reply when he was asked if he had seen the Great Wall: 'Seen it?' he replied.'We were bending free kicks around it!'

Lovely. I like Ron, and think he has proved himself to be an excellent manager. His extravagant style, his hand-made shirts and suits, his jewellery and hairstyle that is now being combed across from under his arm into a huge quiff that a native of Hawaii could surf down – all of those things have made him heaven-sent for a football speaker like myself. John Bond, Tommy Docherty, Peter Swales – all high-profile personalities – are also among those that I have a little go at from time to time during my speeches, but only because I know them, respect them for what they have achieved in the game and, above all, know that every one of them is a true football-lover. The public either love 'em or hate 'em. There are no half measures with men like them. They are people who stand up and do and say exactly what they think, and nobody can deny them the right because they really do love the game. The more characters there are in the game the better it is for everybody. Especially me – they make my job so much easier!

CHAPTER 22

Keeping it in the family

My son Steven, meanwhile, had continued to splutter along in the game, learning all the time. He was quick to realize that, as well as being one of the most enjoyable ways of earning a living, football really is one of the hardest professions in the world.

He served his apprenticeship with Burnley and eventually turned professional with Wigan Athletic, but has already suffered enough heartache and has been dealt enough blows to last him a lifetime. But, like me, he loves every minute of it and keeps coming back for more.

It is amazing, nowadays, how many sons of former players are trying to make their way in football. As I travel around watching Steve play, I see ex-England centre forward Peter Withe watching his son Jason, Walter Joyce and son Warren at Preston. Jim Thompson, the former Rochdale and Exeter City left half, is the proud father of Bolton's midfield star Steve. Terry and Mark Cooper are at Exeter City; Paul Moulden's old man Tony is a former team-mate of mine. Then, in recent years, there has been the Clarke family – Allan, Frank and Wayne – the Allen family of Paul, Clive, Martin and Bradley; and the Wilkins family – Ray and Co. They are all sons of footballing fathers. It sounds like an edition of *Family Fortunes*!

From even further back there were Ken and Peter Barnes at Manchester City, the two Johnny Astons at Manchester United, the two Alan Balls, while Mike Summerbee's son Nicky is at Swindon trying to emulate not only his father but also his grandad George.

The names Gemmill and Bowyer are now appearing regularly on the team-sheet, alongside the name of Clough at Nottingham Forest. They are the offspring of three super ex-players who, each in their own way, brought glory to the City Ground. If these kids achieve half as much success as their famous parents, then the future of Nottingham Forest is indeed in good hands.

Steven, on the other hand, did not have such a hard act to follow. My only ambition for him as a footballer was for him to become a better player than I was. He passed that milestone at about the age of 12, so really anything that happens to him from that point I regard as a bonus.

It is probably something in the jeans(!) that produces footballing families. Certainly, in our case, Judith was a very good player! But it is true to say that any impressionable kid who is lucky enough to have a professional footballer for a father, and goes along to the ground with him from an early age, soaking up the atmosphere of the dressing room, mingling, meeting and watching star players that their school pals can see only on their television screens, is bound to become interested and encouraged to go out into the park when they get home, to try to put into practice what they have seen their father and his famous team-mates doing earlier in the day.

At Manchester City, Johnny Hart was my coach, and his two sons, Paul and Nigel, both developed into two of the most 'professional', professional footballers that I have ever dealt with. And I am sure that the extra edge that they both possess is because they have

162

been brought up in a household that discussed little else besides football.

Once a player crosses that white touchline, he is on his own and no matter who his father is, the road to the top is still a rocky one, and it seems to be no shorter these days than it was in my day, when to me it seemed uphill all the way and a million miles long. For some talented youngsters, however, one quick turn up the right slip road at the correct moment brings them nicely onto the motorway to stardom. For them, the world must seem a wonderful place in which to live and to play football.

Good luck to any kid who tries his luck in professional football. Many are called, but few are chosen. Certainly it is better to have tried and failed, than never to have tried at all. As I watch the game nowadays, I still look, listen and learn, and I realize that while the game is more streamlined, more tactical and ten times as fast as it used to be, not much else changes. Certainly not as regards the treatment of young players; they are still on the receiving end of abuse and bad advice that could scar them for life. That particular aspect of the game seems as bad today as it ever was.

I was watching from the touchline one day and saw a young 15-year-old boy play his first game for his club. He was blond and frail. He was outgrowing his strength and looked like Bambi in a football kit. He seemed as nervous as a kitten, blinking every couple of seconds as he patrolled the left touchline where his coach was standing. He looked completely out of his depth at this level. But I had seen him play before and knew that he possessed a bit of talent. However, this standard was obviously a little too high for him at the moment. It had come too early for him.

After about five or six minutes, the keeper gathered a cross from his right and, in the correct manner, looked up and threw the ball out, quickly and crisply, to the young lad on the left wing, while the opposing full back moved in to close him down. It was a good throw, the correct throw. But the youngster was so nervous that the ball, with what should have been his first touch, flew under his feet and out for a throw-in. The coach completely ignored the young lad, who was only four feet away from him, and screamed at the goalkeeper in a voice that could be heard in Southampton: 'Don't throw it to him, you know he can't play.'

The kid's mother, about 20 yards along the same touchline, ran off and spent the remainder of the game sitting in her car crying her eyes out. Surely that cannot be right. I am sure that they do not teach coaches that sort of thing at Lilleshall. I am not soft by any means, and I have been on the receiving end of quite a few verbal lashings in my time – the way that I played the game, that was inevitable – but not the sort of stuff that reduced me to tears. In fact, it was usually the other way round: I reduced the coaches to tears. These days, however, it would appear that the ability to soak up a good bollocking is as important as being able to control and pass the ball.

Of course, Steven has had to endure his fair share of traumas. That was only to be expected, but what we did not expect was just how difficult he would find it to adjust to the life of a professional footballer. It was the one thing that he had always wanted to do and, although we thought that leaving home and living in lodgings might prove a bit of a problem, he settled into the Pilkington household in Padiham wonderfully well and Gordon and Ellen treated him like a son.

Steve's problems were with the club itself and, eventually, things became so bad that he announced one Sunday evening that he was going to see his immediate boss, Leighton James, at the end of the week and would tell him that he was leaving the club and definitely would not be coming back. Things must have been pretty grim for him to turn his back on the very thing that he had strived and battled for, for so long. But, no matter how much we reasoned with him, talked to him, bullied him, cajoled him, pleaded with him, his mind was made up.

I was very disappointed. I knew that he was making a big mistake, but he was so desperately unhappy that there was absolutely nothing that I could do to make him change his mind. Throughout his last week in Burnley, I dreaded every evening at 6pm when he would ring up and tell us the events of the day.

That week I bumped into Bert Stewart, the father of striker Paul, who, only weeks earlier, had been transferred to Tottenham Hotspur from Manchester City for a massive £1.8 million. Steve, although he had never actually met him, idolized Paul Stewart. Bert asked me how Steve was enjoying life at Burnley and looked as concerned as I was when I told him the horror story. We went on to discuss Paul's fabulous move to Spurs and the good life in division one, before going our separate ways.

The next evening, Steven was sitting miserably in the lounge of Gordon and Ellen's cottage in Padiham, deep in the heart of east Lancashire, contemplating his meeting with Leighton James the following day, when the telephone rang. Gordon answered it and said: 'It's Paul Stewart for you, Tottenham Hotspur.'

Paul, one of football's most expensive stars, had been speaking to his father and, having heard Steven's story, had taken the trouble to find the address of Steven's digs, located the telephone number and dialled a young unknown kid at the other end of the country, simply to talk some sense into him and keep him in the game. He told Steven that he too was finding it difficult to settle down, even with his experience, and that things were even more harrowing for him, living in an hotel in Essex while his wife and young baby were 300 miles away in St Annes. To make matters worse, he had Paul Gascoigne two doors down the corridor in the same hotel, driving him mad every minute of the day and night! He gave Steve the telephone number of the hotel and his room number and said that he must ring him any time, day or night, if ever he wanted to chat about his game, but that under no circumstances must he go and see Leighton James the next morning and pack the game in.

Paul Stewart succeeded where I had failed. On his advice, Steve sorted out the problem for himself and Paul Stewart has acquired for himself the entire Eyre family as lifelong members of the Paul Stewart Fan Club. He would have to commit murder now, before any of us would listen to a bad word said about him.

So, as you can imagine, it really pleases me that he is doing so well at the very top level. Anybody in his position who would go to so much trouble to help a young boy at the very bottom deserves all the success that comes his way. It was not long, however, before I realized that Steven's chances could well be limited when, soon afterwards, there was a change of management at Burnley. Even though it was the manager of the club, Brian Miller, who stepped down to the position of chief scout, it was Steven's mentor, Leighton James, who eventually lost his job as youth team coach in the general re-shuffle that saw Frank Casper appointed as the new manager.

This was Frank's second spell in charge of the club. He had been manager once before and Burnley were now in the unique position of having two people on the staff, Casper and Brian Miller, who had each been the manager of the club on two occasions, and yet were both still employed by the club. They were joined by Arthur Bellamy, in his new capacity as youth team coach. Arthur had on two occasions been assistant manager and recently, during John Bond's reign, had been employed as the groundsman at the club's training ground. It was a strange set-up by anybody's standards. Michael Docherty had also joined the club as assistant manager and I was able to sleep soundly in my bed at night, safe in the knowledge that I had placed my son in the hands of a staff that consisted of a couple of shrewd judges, one of whom had been partly responsible for deciding that Lee Dixon would never make the grade and another one who had, at one time, sent Chris Waddle back to the sausage factory. At a current market value of about £5 million for the pair, they are the sort of decisions to leave off any self-respecting curriculum vitae!

I felt that Steve's all-round play had been improving quite nicely and Leighton James's abrasive tongue had made him tough enough both physically and mentally for him to hold down a regular place in the club's youth team. But I was not convinced that the changes in personnel would work in his favour, although there was, of course, the distinct possibility that he could suffer the same fate as Messrs Dixon and Waddle and be sent on his way, deemed not quite good enough. Mind you, if that was to be the case, it could possibly be regarded as something of a bonus!

CHAPTER 23

The Professional Footballers' Association

Footballers are different things to different people. To the fans on the terracing, they are gods, superstars who can do no wrong. To some outsiders, with no more than a passing interest, they are self-centred individuals who take out plenty but put very little back into the game. To those who are not interested in the sport at all, they are simply a bunch of highly paid individuals who turn up to the ground on Saturdays, chew gum and spit every time the television camera zooms in on them for a close-up.

To me, though, footballers are super people. They are a collection of complex characters from different upbringings, brought together by the common fact that most of them can kick and pass a football with some degree of accuracy. It is true that one or two would not pass the entrance examination for Mensa, or any other exam for that matter. They have, however, learned at the University of Life and developed a streetwise ability, sheer animal cunning and resilience which would get them through most situations with honours.

As soon as a player arrives as a groundstaff lad, apprentice or YTS trainee (the name has changed from era to era, but the principle remains the same), life as a

168

footballer becomes a severe examination of their ability to cope with setbacks that, for some, seem to pile one on top of another like a club sandwich.

Injuries are a problem. So too is a sudden loss of form when, no matter how hard you try, or how much extra training you put in, nothing seems to go your way. Or you can find yourself placed in the hands of a coach who everybody in the game seems to laugh at whenever his name is mentioned, but who, for some inexplicable reason, has managed to secure the job, while dozens of more capable coaches sit at home twiddling their thumbs.

They are all obstacles that you either overcome or that force you out of the race and you fall by the wayside. It is hardly surprising then, that if a player does eventually break through into the big time, against all the odds, he makes the club suffer a bit with his demands when he sits at the boardroom table to discuss his next contract.

American comedienne Joan Rivers says that some of the outrageous contractual demands that she makes, now that she is a world-famous star, are for things that she does not need or will not even take advantage of. But she insists on them as a form of recompense for all the heartache she suffered from two-bit agents, dodgy theatre and club managers and for the mountain of humble pie she was forced to swallow on the way up. Good luck to her, she has paid her dues and so too have most of the players.

Footballers, it is often said, could not pick the winner in a one-horse race. Maybe Stan Bowles, Don Shanks, Kerry Dixon, Mickey Quinn, Channon and Ball, and one or two other famous footballing punters, would not agree with that, but the one thing that footballers do excel at is choosing their own representatives. They are top-class at recognizing the correct men to look after their own interests and the interests of football in general. So when it comes to electing their own chairman of the Professional Footballers' Association from within their own ranks, they have got it right every single time without fail.

Jimmy Hill, who is not everybody's cup of tea as a TV pundit, or as a football club chairman for that matter, was the correct, larger-than-life personality for the job when the players fought for the abolition of the maximum wage. He relished the challenge and was prepared to battle publicly every inch of the way to win a better deal for footballers and, at the same time, carve out a reputation for himself ... and why not? (A little Barry Norman impression thrown in here for good measure!) I have met Jimmy Hill and, believe me, he really looks like he does on TV. If only I had met him a bit earlier, I could have saved myself hours of twiddling the vertical hold on our television at home!

Derek Dougan, another born leader, was also an inspired choice. A colourful character with a touch of the blarney, he could trade verbal punches with the best of them, and he needed all of his vocal dexterity as he led his players towards freedom of contract

Terry Neill, another Irishman with a nice turn of phrase, Steve Coppell (young, bright, with a degree), Alan Gowling, Brian Talbot, Garth Crooks and now Brian Marwood – they are all capable young men, articulate, deep-thinking and caring people. Each one was selected by the players themselves, because they recognized the qualities required, simply by playing with or against them over a number of years.

Secretary Cliff Lloyd did a tremendous job during his long term of office, guiding the game and his members through many traumatic episodes and it was thought that he would be impossible to replace when he eventually retired. But the players unearthed a nugget when they elected Gordon Taylor.

Gordon, from Ashton-under-Lyne, was a left winger

(position, not necessarily political!) during his playing career of 529 games for the four 'B's: Bolton Wanderers, Birmingham City, Blackburn Rovers and Bury. He was a difficult little 'B' to play against as well! Invariably, he was my direct opponent in the reserve teams whenever Manchester City played Bolton Wanderers and, while he usually made life a little uncomfortable for me, he seemed a really nice lad, and we always made a point of having a little chat at the end of the game.

I remember one match in particular at Bromwich Street, Bolton's training ground. It was Easter and games against Wanderers were never easy in those days, because they had such good young players. Dave Lennard was playing left half, Brian Bromley was at inside right, John Hulme was centre half and big Eric Redrobe, an awesome sight in full flight, was playing centre forward against my pal Mike Harold. Eric used to put the fear of God into most defenders. He only played four times for Bolton's first team, but rattled up over 250 games for Southport and Hereford United, rattled in 73 goals and generally rattled the teeth of every centre half that he came in contact with.

I was perfectly happy to be marking little Gordon this day, leaving Mad Eric, in particularly menacing mood, to Mike Harold, who was finding him a bit of a handful to say the least. Late in the second half, we cleared the ball upfield and sprinted out of the penalty area after it in the time-honoured fashion, so that if the ball was played back quickly, we could catch some poor unsuspecting forward offside, if he had been too lazy to run back with us.

Sure enough, our forwards lost possession of the ball – as usual – and it was punted hopefully back into our penalty area. The only person within 40 yards of the ball, except for our goalkeeper, was centre half Mike Harold. He had forgotten the script and had not

171

sprinted out like the rest of us. Fortunately for him, Bolton did not have a lazy forward line – they were all back on the halfway line with us. We turned and watched Mike, all on his own, completely unchallenged, trap the ball beautifully in his own penalty area. Then he bent down slowly, picked the ball up, handed it to the referee with one hand and shook his hand with the other.

I remember Gordon Taylor asking me in amazement what he was doing.

'I know the boss told him at half time to pick up any loose balls down the middle, but this is ridiculous,' I replied.

The referee took the ball from him and apologetically placed it on the penalty spot. Mike's face turned scarlet. I do not know if he and Eric had suffered a clash of heads earlier in the game, but Mike obviously thought that he had heard a whistle blow. Eric Redrobe gratefully hammered home the penalty and we lost the game.

Gordon and I reminisced about this game, and others from the past, as we enjoyed a cup of coffee together many years later in a little bistro just off St Ann's Square in Manchester. We had both retired from the game. I had my stationery business, just around the corner from where we were sitting, and Gordon was now the much-respected secretary of the Professional Footballers' Association.

He had emerged as a fine ambassador for football and had proved conclusively that a footballer's brains are not solely confined to his feet. He has become a man who represents his members not only eloquently and diplomatically, but also with dignity and an understanding of both sides of any issue. Nowadays I think it is fair to say that he is one of the finest football legislators that there has ever been.

'You seem to be doing very well with your after-dinner speaking,' he remarked casually. 'You would be the ideal man to speak at our dinner.'

The PFA Dinner in London is the Cup final of dinners as far as sporting, particularly football, speakers are concerned. It is a glittering affair, which I have attended every year since the very first one in 1974, when Miss Hardman, Cliff Lloyd's secretary, gave me ticket number 0001. The first ticket to the PFA Dinner – I think that is just about the only time that I have ever been first at anything in my life!

Leeds United's Norman Hunter won the Player of the Year award that first time. Since then the event has blossomed into the magnificent affair that it is today. It is a major occasion in the football calendar that is not only attended by most of the professional footballers in this country, but also by many stars from the world of entertainment who come along as invited guests.

Some of Britain's top speakers and comedians have been the main speaker at the PFA Dinner, and it was very flattering for Gordon to mention my name in the same breath. However, I thought that he was merely offering his own opinion. I did not realize that he had specifically invited me out to the bistro to officially ask me to be their guest speaker.

I twiddled with the red and white chequered table cloth, chinked the salt and pepper set together and said with a sigh: 'Yes, it would be nice I must admit, but I doubt if I will ever be thought of in that bracket. You would always have to invite somebody really well-known to speak at a dinner as grand as yours.'

Gordon never mentioned it again. I did not realize that I had turned him down, because I did not think that I had been asked in the first place, and it was two years before the subject was raised again.

The Football Writers' Dinner is the long-established event when the Footballer of the Year is crowned. This coveted award is voted for by football's journalists and some of the biggest names in football such as Johnny Carey, Stanley Matthews, Bert Trautmann, Danny Blanchflower, Joe Mercer, Dave Mackay and many more, have received the lovely statuette that accompanies the honour. This particular year Gary Lineker was to receive it and I was to be the guest speaker.

It was the Thursday morning prior to the all-Mersey FA Cup final, Liverpool v Everton, and Bob Cass, chairman for the year, had obviously given the official proceedings and entertainment a lot of thought. As well as persuading me to speak, he had also invited, as the comedian for the evening, Spike Rawlings.

Spike, a comic from the north-east, just happened to be the same Spike Rawlingson who, in his younger days, as a giant centre half for Bury, had tackled my good self, playing right half for Manchester City, with such ferocity that I left the scene of the crime on a stretcher and never pulled on a sky-blue shirt again. That sure was some tackle! I finished up in wards four, five and six. But, to be fair, it was not a foul – it just felt to me as though I had been hit by the 5.30 train from Euston, and it was probably my own fault that I did not simply jump out of the way.

On his retirement, Spike took a job as a lumberjack, scything down trees by tackling them the same way as he had tackled me! He then began touring the tough north-east circuit of working men's clubs, making the blokes laugh after their game of dominoes and threatening to slide tackle any who did not.

Bob Cass, ever the sentimentalist, thought that it would be a novel idea to organize a touching reunion by inviting us both to entertain the troops at the dinner. It is still the only time that I have ever worn shin-pads underneath my dinner suit!

The evening, it has to be said, was an unqualified success. The audience seemed to enjoy my part of it and we all found Spike very funny indeed ... certainly a lot more humorous than the last time we had met! One of the many people to congratulate me at the end was Gordon Taylor.

'Well done,' he said. 'Absolutely brilliant! But I can't understand why you agreed to do the Football Writers' Dinner, but you turned the PFA down. They are both equally big events ... and you were a player yourself, after all.'

I was a little shocked ... he had missed out the word 'bad' before he said 'player'!

'I've never been asked,' I protested, and Gordon then reminded me about our little tête-à-tête in the bistro.

I assured him that it was not intended as a snub. I would not knowingly turn down Gordon Taylor for anything and agreed, there and then, to be the next speaker at the PFA Dinner ... provided that I was not in the running for the award myself!

CHAPTER 24

Look who's coming to dinner

The Professional Footballers' Association Dinner is always a tremendous success. The magnitude of the occasion, the pomp and circumstance, the fanfare of trumpets before each item on the agenda, the official toastmaster in full regalia and the magnificent splendour of the venue all go together to ensure that the evening is one to remember for everybody who attends – especially if you are fortunate enough to be one of the players who receives an award. There must be no finer sense of achievement for anybody than to be voted the best in your chosen profession by your peers, the very people against whom you compete week in and week out.

It has to be said, however, that, as a veteran of every PFA Dinner so far, I have seen some of our very top entertainers struggle to make an impact with an audience of over a thousand footballers, all gathered together under one roof. Because of that, the prospect of faring the same way flitted in and out of my head with worrying regularity in the weeks leading up to the event.

As everyone knows, footballers love a night out when they can get together for a laugh or for a gossip to compare wage packets, and this occasion is the ideal opportunity for them to enjoy themselves, which they always do. So I can never understand why the speaker so often comes unstuck.

Of course, not everybody has a hard time. In the early days, an almost unknown Jasper Carrott did very well. Bernard Manning, as usual, tore the place apart. Stan Boardman, after a dodgy start when the Italian sponsors did not seem to appreciate one or two little jokes at their expense, was able to draw upon his vast experience of manoeuvring his way around tricky situations by changing tack in mid-act. He concentrated instead on the 'Geermans' and so finished on a high note. My pal Johnny Kennedy took a gamble by deciding to move about among the vast audience of stars with a portable microphone and generally took the mickey out of any unfortunate individual who fell under his gaze. It came off for him too.

Despite this, over the years I felt that too many experienced speakers had not really done themselves justice and that pretty soon it would be my turn and there was no way that I was going to suffer the same way, if there was anything, in terms of preparation, that I could possibly do to avoid it. With this in mind, I spent a long time deciding just what I was and was not going to say. After Stan's experience, however, whoever the sponsors were I was going to leave them alone.

Eventually, the big day arrived, a beautiful April Sunday morning, and I set off from Manchester, stopping only to pick up my two guests, Stewart and Glen, plus David White and Steve Redmond, two of Manchester City's promising young players. I had promised the two boys a lift to London where they were to link up with the England Under-21 team.

The Grosvenor House Hotel in Park Lane is a magnificent building; opulence pours out of every nook and cranny. After depositing my luggage and hanging up my dinner suit in my suite, I then set about making my first mistake. I decided to wander down to the banqueting hall to inspect the room, test the microphone and get the feel and ambience of the place ... I wish that I had not bothered. The empty room seemed enormous. It was hard to imagine that my voice could possibly carry to all four corners, even with the very best sound equipment. In fact, there were probably one or two guests who hoped that it would not! Everything was beautifully set out in preparation for the event: table plans, waiters scurrying about putting the finishing touches to this masterpiece, the massive top table looked like the setting for the Last Supper (and, with one or two of those old codgers from the FA up there, it occurred to me that the players might think that it was with the original cast!).

I strolled over to the top table, located my place setting in the middle, surveyed the scene, and it looked no less imposing from there. This was definitely going to be a lot different to calling out the bingo numbers at the White Moss Pensioners' Christmas Party.

Later on, resplendent in my dinner suit, I walked down the spiral staircase like Blake Carrington (no! not wearing a wig!) looking the picture of elegance and confidence, until I squeezed past the Millwall table.

'Are you the speaker tonight, mate?' enquired a Cockney voice that had probably been selling jellied eels earlier in the day. 'I've read all of your books.'

'Thanks very much,' I replied with my sweetest smile.

'Crap!' he said.

It was my own fault for assuming that, just because he had read them, he had enjoyed them. Another lesson learned the hard way. Would this be a foretaste of things to come?

When everybody was finally assembled, the top table guests made their grand entrance. It made a pleasant change for me to be clapped in – usually I am clapped out at that time of night! I shuffled my way past the place cards that looked like a who's who of English soccer, until I reached my place. I was next to the three Bobbys – Robson, Charlton and Davro. Bobby Davro was due to wind up the evening's entertainment with a few of the impressions that had made him such a big TV star.

I became quite misty-eyed as I surveyed the scene. It was an awesome sight: 1,300 bow ties – probably the biggest crowd that I had ever appeared in front of … and that includes my playing days! Wherever I looked, my eye fell upon a famous face from one era or another. I should really have been concentrating on the job in hand but, seeing those super players again made me realize that I have been one of the fortunate ones to have either watched or played football over five decades.

I was born just in time to remember Frank Swift, flat caps and the massive crowds of the late 1940s, the days when you arrived at the ground at least two hours before the kick-off so that you could be sure of claiming your favourite spot. I could walk blindfolded into Maine Road in those days and still find my way to the same few inches of terracing where I always used to stand come rain, hail or snow, just to the side of the goal at the scoreboard end.

It is fun now, of course, to see computerized little men jumping up and down shouting 'Goal' on electronic scoreboards up and down the country, as the half-time scores are flashed up on the screens almost as soon as the referees have blown their whistle. But it does not have quite the same magic as the little old man in the rickety old scoreboard waiting for the scores to be telephoned through from around the country, then hoisting those cumbersome old metal numbers onto their hinges, while we all held our breath to see if United were losing.

I was lucky to have had the opportunity to admire the skills of Matthews, Finney, Real Madrid, Duncan Edwards and the Busby Babes in the 1950s, and to see Law, Best, Charlton, Moore and Pele all at their peak in the 'Swinging Sixties', when the crowd still used to applaud the players at the end of the game, instead of the other way round. The 1970s brought a different breed of star, but Francis Lee, Peter Thompson of Liverpool, Kevin Keegan and Johan Cruyff were still a joy to watch and, in the 1980s, Glenn Hoddle, Bryan Robson, Kenny Dalglish, Ian Rush and Gary Lineker have proved themselves to be supreme exponents of a game that has advanced, both tactically and physically, so much in recent years that it is almost frightening.

I have witnessed all of the significant changes: I have seen the 'Wingless Wonders', 'total football', the Revie Plan, 4-3-3, 4-4-2, 9-0-1, 10-Jack-Queen-King! And, of course, I saw the good old English formation, when we ruled the world, of 'two full backs, three half backs and five for'ads', as the Lion of Vienna, Nat Lofthouse, so beautifully puts it.

I have seen players funnelling, fannying and grovelling. I have seen them overlapping, hitting space, making space and marking space, but what is his opponent doing while he is marking space?

Players are told to 'Hit the channel! Hit the channel!'

'What d'ya think I am – a bleedin' swimmer?'

'We'll soon find out. Get in the bath!'

Some things never change. The coach always has the final word.

No longer does the Number 3 simply mark the Number 7 and patrol his own patch, waiting either to kill or be killed. The days when full backs chipped crippled wingers across the field to one another are long gone. They are now super-fit athletes, expected to attack and defend with equal expertise, cross beautiful

180

balls from the flanks and chip in with a few goals a season for good measure. If a full back scored more than half a dozen goals in his entire playing career in the 1940s, 1950s or 1960s he was regarded as something of a phenomenon. Players like Peter Baker and Ron Henry, the full-back pair in the fabulous Spurs team that won the Cup and league double in 1961, played 556 games between them and scored a total of four goals: three for Baker (who was obviously a lot more attack minded!) and one for Henry. That is some record, but they were both vital members of that all-conquering team, indeed Ron Henry picked up an England cap along the way.

It was particularly thrilling for me to see so many great players tucking into their gourmet food, but it did little to ease my nerves. And if I expected to gain solace from an experienced artiste like Bobby Davro, I was sadly disappointed, because he seemed a little jumpy as well as he nervously pushed his food around his plate. He mumbled that his choice of impressions would be limited, because he had neither props, make-up nor music. Come to think of it, neither did I. Our confidence was not boosted when we sat back and listened to chairman Brian Talbot fight a losing battle to make himself heard over the din of a crowd which, for some reason, simply refused to quieten down.

As if all this was not enough, Bobby Charlton was sitting next but one to me, blissfully unaware that he was giving me another problem to contend with. I always start my speech with a little derogatory remark about Manchester United. It is only a bit of harmless fun just to let everybody know that I am from the blue half of Manchester. But I did not feel comfortable about doing it while Bobby Charlton was sitting so close.

Actually Bobby was not the real problem. I like Bobby and I know that he possesses a keen sense of humour when he lets the mask slip, and he does not mind a joke at his own expense so long as it is delivered with a touch of respect. But I knew inwardly that the moment I mentioned Manchester United, 1,300 pairs of eyes would instantly flick towards United's favourite son and, if he did not approve, then they too would not laugh and, after a bad start like that, I would probably never recover from it. I do not know any German jokes to fall back on like Stan Boardman!

So, there and then, I decided to leave out the line and start my speech another way, but the more I thought about it, the more I realized that tonight, above all other nights, I needed my usual opening. I'll leave it in, I thought, and hope that Bobby is in a jovial mood. I leaned across Bobby Davro and said chirpily to Mr Charlton: 'Did you enjoy the game yesterday, Bobby?'

He wrinkled his nose and, without looking up from his plate, replied that he had not much liked it.

Bloody hell! I thought. I will leave it out!

That was how it went throughout the meal: that opening line was in and out quicker than a David Gower innings! Eventually I noticed Gary Mabbutt, obviously enjoying himself at a table situated right in front of me. He is a lovely lad, the type you would not object to your daughter bringing home for tea on a Sunday afternoon, his happy, open, smiling face made me think that it did not have to be Manchester United, it could be Spurs.

So I decided to change it to Tottenham Hotspur and leave the line in. After much toing and froing, I had made up my mind – my indecision was now final!

Meanwhile, total chaos had broken out during the latest speech, and my heart went out to Bobby Robson who, for some inexplicable reason, was the butt of some form of demonstration by a group of people who were obviously not footballers.

It took quite a while before some order could be

restored to the proceedings. I must admit that I was shocked at the lack of respect shown to the England manager and also to Brian Talbot, who were both speaking in their official capacities as football administrators. As Bobby Davro and I had both been invited along to entertain the audience, we were fair game, but it was quite alarming to think that the hooligan element that was infesting the terraces had somehow infiltrated into this showpiece footballing occasion and causing difficulties for these leading characters from the sport.

All of which was no consolation to me, a humble Blackley boy, who was just about to stand up and do his best. It was a nasty situation all round and one that could quite easily turn into a nightmare. I thought that if the toastmaster gave me a fairly long introduction that might give the rabble a chance to quieten down, so I beckoned him across and asked him if he would be good enough to help me out. From out of the corner of his mouth (he obviously used to play left back in a blow football team!) he whispered, quite emphatically, just two words: 'No, sir.'

He could have said two other words, the second one being 'off', and it would have amounted to the same thing. At least he was polite about it and he showed that he was indeed a man of few words when it came to the actual introduction because, after a fanfare of trumpets, he simply said 'Fred Eyre'. And from that point onwards, I was definitely on my own.

Normally, when I first stand up, the faces in the audience are a blur, but not tonight. I could see everybody crystal clear. I knew just where everybody was seated. I glanced at Gary Mabbutt and then launched into my attack on his team, Tottenham Hotspur. Gary laughed louder than anybody, with the possible exception of Bobby Charlton – little did he know! I was off to a great start and, from that point, I never looked back.

The wisdom of my little gamble was proved a little later on when Bobby Davro eventually got to his feet and began by telling the audience how unlucky he had always been in life: 'Treets melt in my hand. I even come from an unlucky family. My uncle was unlucky; he went for a hair transplant and then found out that the donor was Bobby Charlton!'

I held my breath, not daring to look at Bobby Charlton. I looked instead at 1,300 pairs of eyes as they flicked in his direction and could tell by the silence that had descended upon the room that Bobby had responded with the same forced smile that I had first seen many years ago when I walked through the streets of Valetta in Malta with him. That day a middle-aged man came rushing up to him carrying the dirtiest, scruffiest little urchin in his arms that it is possible to imagine. The young boy was holding an ice cream that had melted in the hot sun. His hands were covered in the stuff and it was running down both arms. He had managed to smear it all over his filthy little face into his hair and into his ears where there was enough dirt to grow a pound of 'King Edwards'.

'Bobbee! Bobbee!' the man shouted, as we both stopped for him to sign the inevitable autograph. Bobby Charlton's patience when signing autographs is really quite unbelievable. He has been a star for so long that he must have made a decision early on in his life never to refuse to sign one and, as far as I know, he never has said 'No' to anybody.

'Please Bobbee, kiss my son,' the man said. Bobby physically blanched at the horrifying prospect, protested a little bit, but then bowed to the inevitable when the man insisted. He gritted his teeth, smiled the smile that I could imagine painted on his face at the Grosvenor House this very minute and puckered up into the sea of vanilla.

Footballers love to laugh at themselves and they

certainly do not mind laughing at the many footballing buffoons in the game, but they do not always laugh at references to their own legends, like Bobby Charlton, and I was pleased with myself that I had switched to Tottenham Hotspur. It proved to be the best free transfer of my career! It gave me the confidence to deliver my speech with as much humour as possible, because that is what is expected from me, but also with as much depth and genuine feeling for the game of football that I could muster.

As I stood there, addressing the best footballers in the country, both past and present, I felt totally justified in being there. I felt that not only was I representing myself, somebody who had achieved very little in terms of success over the years but had worked very hard simply to remain in the game. But I felt that I was also representing many more hundreds and thousands of players who played the game, gave it their best shot, but never achieved the stardom enjoyed by the players in this audience. They remained in love with football nevertheless, because, much as we all admire them, the game is not all about star players.

As the entire room rose to its feet to give me a marvellous ovation (thank you Graham Rix and Trevor Morgan for being the first to stand up: was it a touch of cramp?), I concluded by saying: 'I realize that, for an evening such as this, the members of the Professional Footballers' Association could have invited anybody in the country to be the main speaker. But they didn't. They asked me ... one of their own ... somebody who is always proud to say that he was once a professional footballer.'

I was not a very good one, but one who always talked a good game. This has enabled me to travel the length and breadth of the United Kingdom, meet nice people and hopefully entertain them a little bit better off the football field than I did when I was trying my very best to perform on it.

Really, there wasn't that much to beat ... was there?